THE BEST OF THE

blues

THE BEST OF THE

blues

The Essential CD Guide

Roger St. Pierre

CollinsPublishersSanFrancisco
A Division of HarperCollins*Publishers*

First published in the United States in 1993 by Collins Publishers San Francisco,
1160 Battery Street, San Francisco, California 94111

Library of Congress Cataloging-in-Publication Data

St. Pierre, Roger.
    The best of the blues : the essential CD guide / Roger St. Pierre.
        p.   cm. — (The Essential CD guides)
    Discography: p.
    Includes index.
    ISBN 0-00-255337-6
    1. Blues musicians—United States—Biography—Dictionaries.
    2. Blues (Music)—History and criticism.   3. Compact discs—Reviews.
I. Title. II. Series.
HL 102.B637 1993
781.643—dc20
                                          93-11544
                                          CIP
                                          MN

Printed in Great Britain

THE AUTHOR

Roger St. Pierre is the blues expert at *Blues & Soul* (UK) magazine. He has
written 27 books, over 1,000 album sleeve notes and is a regular contributor
to many popular-music magazines. He was also the main contributor to the
bestselling *Harmony Illustrated Encyclopedia of Rock* (published by Harmony)

Contents

INTRODUCTION

America's Greatest Art Form

The Sound Which Inspired the World

BLACK AMERICA'S GREATEST GIFT TO THE WORLD, THE BLUES IS THE UNDERPINNING OF ALMOST ALL TODAY'S POPULAR MUSIC. FROM THE RAW POWER OF HEAVY METAL TO THE SMOOTH SOPHISTICATION OF POP SOUL, FROM THE STREET-HIP RAP TO THE INFECTIOUSNESS OF REGGAE AND THE ROCK PLAYED BY BANDS FROM MOSCOW TO SYDNEY, THE BLUES INFLUENCE IS ALL-PERVASIVE.

The blues has touched jazz and even classical music, as can be detected through the works of both Delius and Dvorak. Even country—once described by B. B. King as "white man's blues"—has felt its impact.

Born of the trials and tribulations, and the rare yet treasured good times, of a people transplanted from Africa to slavery in a strange new land, the blues has become true world music, reaching out and touching the emotions of us all. Its exponents now include not only white as well as black Americans but Europeans and others too. And, thanks to this new dimension, a music which only a few years ago seemed destined to become a mere museum piece has been given a potent rebirth. The black American community, which had turned its back on the blues in favour of soul and funk, is now rediscovering its rich heritage and a new generation of younger players, spearheaded by Robert Cray, is injecting renewed vitality into the form.

While we have bid farewell to the likes of Muddy Waters, Elmore James and Howlin' Wolf, their seminal music lives on through their recordings and such long-time stalwarts as B. B. King—still maintaining a gruelling schedule of nearly 350 concerts a year—and John Lee Hooker—the oldest artist ever to grace the highest echelons of the album charts—go on from strength to strength.

Surely, there is no art form quite as evocative as the classic 12-bar with its haunting call-and-response patterns. This book is a celebration of the music and the people who made and continue to make it.

It was once jokingly said that you could dial almost any number in the Memphis telephone directory and have a strong chance of finding a blues singer at the other end of the line—and that's not so far from the truth. Traditionally, the blues was very much the people's music, and those who could not afford proper instruments would improvise or simply sing a cappella: "When I was growing up in the South, you sang gospel in church on a Sunday and blues on the back porch every evening," recalls B. B. King.

Given such a vast pool of talent, no wonder so much truly great music emerged. And, thankfully, a huge amount of it found its way on to record—and was given rack space, not just in specialist R&B shops in the black communities of its native land but in record stores around the world.

Such has been the universal acceptance of blues, particularly since the great explosions of interest during the blues booms of the Sixties, Seventies and early Nineties, that even the most obscure of releases stands a good chance of being issued in any number of foreign territories.

The sterling work of blues buff researchers and discographers, of enthusiasts on the staff of major record companies and of those behind such specialist revival labels as Delmark, Alligator, Ichiban, Black Top, Sonet, Sequel, Charly, Ace, Arhoolie, Topic and Indigo have all helped to keep the flow of good music coming, both with reissues and new recordings.

But perhaps the nicest thing about it all is the knowledge that the best of the blues is not an esoteric music whose potential appeal is limited to diehard collectors only. Much of it, given the right level of exposure, could even today earn itself a place in the pop music charts—as proven by the success of John Lee Hooker's 'Boom Boom' remake.

That crossover success is more than possible is evidenced by the enormous reaction when an obscure old Champion Jack Dupree "walking blues" number titled 'Mother In Law Blues' was lifted from a late night blues show and given a Sunday lunchtime prime spot airing on a family programme. The radio station concerned had its phones jammed with calls from little old ladies, and youngsters too, who wanted to know the title of "that nice record".

This book is designed not only to help such newcomers open the wondrous treasure chest which is the world of blues music but also to provide an informative reference source to those already committed to this most fascinating genre.

To tell this story, we have, as objectively as possible, made our own selection of 10 legends and 100 other major artists, as well as a purely personal choice of favourite classic recordings. While we are sure readers will not argue with any of our choices, they may well feel that there are others who equally merited inclusion.

So, to fans of such artists as Furry Lewis, Gus Cannon, Matt Murphy, Juke Boy Bonner, Blind Boy Fuller, Z. Z. Hill, Robert Lockwood Jr., Eddie Kirkland, Floyd Jones, Canned Heat, Papa Lightfoot, Charlie "Papa" Jackson, Arthur Gunter, Jazz Gillum, George "Honeyboy" Edwards, Tiny Bradshaw, Ruth Brown, Josh White, Papa John Creach, J. B. Hutto, Johnny Adams, Stevie Ray Vaughn, Don "Sugarcane" Harris, Hammie Nixon, Bukka White and the many others who have written their own page in the blues story, we can only offer apologies for their omission and plead "pressure of space".

CHICAGO and the NORTH

The Strident Sound of the Big City

*W*HEN ROBERT JOHNSON, THE ENIGMATIC "KING OF THE DELTA BLUES", WROTE AND SANG 'SWEET HOME CHICAGO', HE WAS ENCAPSULATING THE DREAMS AND ASPIRATIONS OF MILLIONS OF POOR SOUTHERN BLACKS WHO SAW THE INDUSTRIAL CITIES OF THE NORTH AS THEIR PROMISED LAND. THE TRAILS FIRST SET BY ESCAPING SLAVES ON THE "UNDERGROUND RAILROAD" BEFORE THE AMERICAN CIVIL WAR HAD BECOME WELL WORN BY THE LATE 1940S. THE STEADY FLOW TURNED INTO A FLOOD.

Naturally, the migrants' music travelled with them. Recording companies like RCA Bluebird and RKO were already finding a rich vein of talent in Chicago's tenement housing back in the Thirties but as the Second World War drew to a close the local recording industry took off with a vengeance.

New arrivals like Muddy Waters, his half-brother Otis Spann, Otis Rush and others provided competition for old hands like Big Bill Broonzy and John Lee "Sonny Boy" Williamson, who had been in town since the mid-Thirties. Where earlier arrivals had replicated the sounds of the South, these newcomers introduced a whole new style, going electric with a vengeance and defining the roots of a sound which would lead via Jimi Hendrix, Eric Clapton and their ilk to the universal heavy rock sound of today.

Even those like B. B. King and the other Sonny Boy Williamson (Rice Miller) who, thanks to their own radio shows, had already built very substantial careers in the South, could not resist the lure of the urban North and all that it promised.

Detroit, whose automobile factories were providing ready employment for the new arrivals, followed the same trend as Chicago, with John Lee Hooker coming in from the Delta and scoring one of black music's very first million-sellers with 'In The Mood', in 1949.

Thanks to the highly active King/Federal group of labels, Cincinnati too was a magnet, providing an outlet for the unrelated Freddie King and Albert King.

But it was Chicago—to this day the undisputed capital of the blues—which attracted the greatest number of aspiring black stars, most of them playing for nickels and dimes on Maxwell Street before graduating to the Southside blues bars.

What had once been dubbed "race music", then "sepia" or "ebony" had, by 1949, earned the definition "rhythm and blues". Electrified and amplified, this took on an altogether more strident, extrovert edge, not to be found in its country blues roots. Songs still tended to be about tough times and lost loves but cars, guns and the other trappings of big city life took the place of mules and ploughs as the artefacts.

Jazz, gospel, doo-wop and the emergent rock 'n' roll and soul music added to Chicago's rich music scene, helped by the presence in the city not only of outposts of the major recording companies but of emergent home-grown independent labels. Cobra, Chief and other small outfits might have lacked big funding, and therefore clout, but proved a ready home for talents like Otis Rush and Magic Sam. Brunswick concentrated on soul but put out some blues sides, as did Mercury. Vee Jay played it across the board—earning million-sellers with truly downhome blues sounds from Jimmy Reed and John Lee Hooker as well as the early hits of not only the Four Seasons but also the Beatles!

Chess and its associated Checker and Cadet labels also offered a kaleidoscope of jazz, soul, gospel and rock 'n' roll. But, thanks to the dynamic recordings of a vast roster which included Muddy Waters, Howlin' Wolf, Sonny Boy Williamson, Buddy Guy, Lowell Fulsom, Jimmy Rodgers, Little Milton, Etta James, Sugar Pie DeSanto, KoKo Taylor, Little Walter, Walter "Shakey" Horton, and many others, the company will always remain synonymous with the blues.

It was no surprise that a number of young local white musicians began hanging out in the Chicago blues clubs and then adopted the sound for themselves—Mike Bloomfield, Paul Butterfield and others going on to become major rock stars.

The deaths of Waters, Wolf, Leonard Chess and other key figures and the selling-off of Chess ended the golden days. But the city continues to play a pivotal role in the blues. A new generation of talents, including Carey Bell, Luther Allison, Billy Boy Arnold and new-wave specialist labels like Delmark and Alligator still call it "Sweet Home Chicago".

THE DELTA

Music from the Rural Roots

*U*NSPECTACULAR, LOW-LYING FARMING COUNTRY, WHERE COTTON WAS ONCE KING, THE MISSISSIPPI DELTA OF BLUES LEGEND IS NOT LOCATED, AS YOU MIGHT EXPECT FROM THE NAME, AT THE POINT WHERE THAT MIGHTY RIVER SPILLS INTO THE GULF OF MEXICO BUT IS TO BE FOUND MANY HUNDREDS OF MILES FURTHER NORTH.

Extending from the suburbs of Memphis, Tennessee, down to Vicksburg, Mississippi, the rich alluvial plain of the Delta country lies between the Mississippi and Yazoo rivers. It is a region where blacks for many years outnumbered whites by two to one. Given that the total population has never exceeded half a million and that none of the Delta's three main towns—Clarksdale, Greenville and Greenwood—has more than 17,000 inhabitants, it is amazing how this seemingly sleepy region has played such a pivotal role in the evolution of a music of universal importance.

Delta blues was nurtured in the field camps and work gangs of the levees and cotton-fields, played live in roadside juke joints and shantytown houseparties. To get on to record, local artists either had to await the arrival of Alan Lomax, Sam Charters or some other field researcher scouring the South with a home tape-recorder, looking for rare sounds, or travel to Memphis or much further afield. And, of course, so many of them—Big Bill Broonzy, Muddy Waters, Howlin' Wolf, John Lee Hooker, the two Sonny Boy Williamsons and others included—never came back home again.

The mysterious Robert Johnson, the uncrowned "King of the Delta Blues", only had two recording sessions—both in far off Texas (the first held in a hotel in San Antonio, the second, seven months later, at a Dallas studio).

This was the land of racism and segregation, of the notorious Parchman State Farm penal colony, of Ku-Klux-Klan terror and fiery crosses. It was a place where blacks broke their backs tilling the lands and where, in fairness, there were many white sharecroppers who were little better off economically—but at least the rednecks had the law on their side.

The twin routes of Highway 51 and Highway 61—the latter immortalized in song by Bob Dylan—plus the parallel railway, link the Delta with Chicago so it is no surprise that more than three-quarters of all the blacks who migrated to the Windy City were natives of Mississippi. Nor is it a surprise that it was the Delta sound which provided the frame

Howlin' Wolf was one of a legion of Delta bluesmen who ended up in Chicago, via Memphis.

work for Chicago's role as blues capital of the world.

Not just bluesmen but other
black recording artists like Sam
Cooke, Bo Diddley, and even Diana
Ross came from families rooted in
the Mississippi Delta country.

The influence of the Delta on
black culture has not been just a
postwar phenomenon. Right from
the early days of blues recording,
singers from the region were captured on disc and popularized among
a far more widespread black audience. Charly Patton, Bukka White,
Son House, Peetie Wheatstraw,
Dave "Honeyboy" Edwards and Big
Joe Williams were just a few of the
itinerant musicians who perambu-
lated through the Delta, playing for
a few dollars—and as much moon-
shine whisky as they could handle.

B. B. King, who was born in
Indianola, Mississippi, remembers his own beginnings,
before fame and for-
tune took him to
Memphis, then

11

Muddy Waters took the haunting Delta sound north to Chicago.

Chicago and on to a worldwide stage: "We'd travel out to the back woods, riding in beaten up old jalopies and play from dusk to sunrise. Those places were real lively. There would often be fights, even stabbings—usually over woman trouble—sadly, but the music was always tremendous. I nearly lost my life in one of those places—it went up in flames and my treasured guitar, Lucille, burned with it", he recalled many years later.

B.B. escaped to buy a new guitar but the juke joints did cost Robert Johnson his life, at the early age of 26—victim of a jealous man who laced his whisky with poison. As he claimed in 'Crossroads', Johnson was said to have already sold his soul to the devil in exchange for the ability to play majestic blues— a trade also supposedly made by Peetie Wheatstraw, a man dubbed "The Devil's Son-in-Law".

In the deeply religious—and superstitious—rural black communities, the performing of blues was held to be the worst of low morals, not surprisingly since most of it was played in places where men fought and even killed over other men's women—"bad liquor, bad women", to quote a popular line. No wonder most of those who performed the music had no roots—sleeping wherever anyone would lend them a bed or a floor for the night: "I'd rather drink muddy water, sleep out in a hollow log/Than to stay in this town, treated like a dirty dog."

It was W. C. Handy, the self-proclaimed "Father of the Blues" who documented hearing an early performance in the Delta idiom while visiting Tutwiler, Mississippi, way back in 1895, and described the musician concerned using the "bottleneck" guitar playing style which was to become the Delta trademark—a bottleneck, steel tube or knife being slid along the strings to produce a sound similar to that achieved by Hawaiian guitarists, but far more haunting.

It was a sound which would be developed to its ultimate by the redoubtable Muddy Waters— acoustically on the epic *Folk Sounds Of* album and with shattering power on his electrically amplified classics for Chess. For it was Waters, who grew up deep in Delta country, who took this ethnic folk music from a remote backwater of the American southlands and transformed it into the strident Chicago urban blues sound which became a clarion call for creative musicians from around the globe, leading to the evolution of rock as we know it today.

MEMPHIS

Beale Street Boogie

*S*TRATEGICALLY PLACED ALONGSIDE THE MIGHTY MISSISSIPPI, HALF WAY BETWEEN NEW ORLEANS AND CHICAGO, MEMPHIS IS A MAJOR COMMUNICATIONS HUB LOCATED WHERE TWO OF THE MAJOR NORTH–SOUTH AND EAST–WEST AXES OF THE USA CROSS EACH OTHER. IT IS UNDERSTANDABLE, THEN, THAT THE CITY HAS LONG BEEN A HOTBED OF MUSICAL ACTIVITY—OF WIDELY DIVERSE TYPES.

Beale Street has been a hotbed of jazz from the early days of that idiom, jug music, country and western and rockabilly also thrive in the city and "the Memphis Sound" revolutionized soul music, thanks to Stax, Hi, Goldwax and the recordings of Otis Redding, Sam and Dave, Eddie Floyd, the MGs, Al Green, Ann Peebles, James Carr and many more.

And Memphis was also, of course, the adopted home of Elvis Presley. Himself a son of the Delta—he was born in Tupelo, Mississippi—Elvis, like so many other youngsters, black and white alike, grew up listening to the rootsy sounds of the blues, courtesy of Sonny Boy Williamson's *King Biscuit Boy* show, beamed out of Helena, Arkansas, and the shows hosted on Memphis-based Radio WDIA by B. B. King and Rufus Thomas.

It was no surprise that "the King" included covers of Arthur "Big Boy" Crudup originals among his early recordings (his first hit being with a version of 'That's Alright Mama'), nor that he signed with Sam Phillips's Sun label. Before launch-

ing the rock 'n' roll revolution, with not only Elvis but also Carl Perkins, Roy Orbison and Jerry Lee Lewis, the astute Phillips had concentrated largely on the blues, recording Rufus Thomas, Little Milton, Howlin' Wolf, Little Junior Parker and Dr Ross among others—often leasing the material to out-of-state labels like Chess (in Chicago) and Modern (in Los Angeles).

Another Memphis-based King—by name, as well as stature—the mesmeric B.B. of that ilk, was first signed to Modern, in a deal put together by Ike Turner. The enigmatic songwriter, keyboard player, guitarist and producer who went on to international stardom with wife Tina, spent the Fifties serving as a talent scout for various record companies, often recording his discoveries in hotel bedrooms (B. B. King's huge-selling '3am Blues' was cut in just this fashion).

Though never actually a member of the group, B.B. served as catalyst for a loose-knit Memphis aggregation known as the Beale Streeters, a perambulating line-up including

In his earlier days, soul star Ike Turner was a catalyst of the Memphis blues scene.

such redoubtable talents as Johnny Ace, Roscoe Gordon, Earl Forrest and Bobby "Blue" Bland.

Like so many of the leading Memphis blues acts, Ace and Bland ended up, along with another Memphis artist, Little Junior Parker, finding fame through a record label based elsewhere. Duke Records had originally been set up in Memphis by a local DJ but he soon sold out to Houston, Texas-based club owner and entrepreneur Don Robey, a man notorious for his tough approach to business.

Ace was set for superstardom, being acclaimed "the most programmed R&B artist of 1954" by *Cashbox* magazine, but his career came to an abrupt and tragic end that Christmas Eve when he shot himself dead while playing Russian roulette backstage at the City Auditorium in Houston.

Bland, in contrast, went on to a career which produced a seemingly non-stop run of R&B chart entries and a prodigious output of albums over the space of more than 40 years—thanks to a highly individual style which comfortably straddled the divide between soul and the blues. After a short stint with the Miniatures' gospel act and fronting the Adolph Duncan Band, Bland worked as B. B. King's chauffeur and valet before finding stardom in his own right.

The lack of success of Bland's early records provoked the comment "he should forget singing and buy himself a plough" from the hard-headed Bihari brothers, who had leased the sides for their Los Angeles-based Modern label. But Bland returned from national service with a new maturity and, backed by a big band directed by trumpeter and arranger Joe Scott and with his vocal gyrations reflected by the superlative guitar work of first Pat Hare then Wayne Bennett, he produced one of the most potently original sounds in black music.

While vocalist Bland and guitarist/singer B. B. King often appeared and recorded together down through the years, guitarist/singer Little Milton managed to sound like them both at one and the same time—yet still maintained an identity of his own. Like King and so many others, Milton eventually moved base to Chicago.

It was a well-trodden path. Unknown artists would come to Memphis from the country districts of Tennessee, Arkansas, Alabama and Mississippi, stay a while, build a reputation, then move north or out to the West Coast. Memphis Slim went even further, shifting his base to Paris where, through the Sixties and early Seventies, he served as a true ambassador of the blues.

Following in Ike Turner's footsteps, some went to St Louis, where the presence of Chuck Berry ensured a lively scene. Berry made his name in rock 'n' roll but also recorded a number of fine blues sides and provided ready employment for blues musicians in his classy band.

By the Seventies, the traffic was running in both directions. Albert King, unrelated to B. B. King but, like him, a native of Indianola, Mississippi, had made his early recordings in Chicago and St Louis, but in the late Sixties he went to Memphis to record prolifically and highly successfully for Stax, a label which strengthened its move into blues territory by also bringing both Little Milton and Jimmy McCracklin into the city. In a park just off Beale Street there is a statue to W. C. Handy, composer of 'St Louis Blues' and billed by Memphis as "the Father of the Blues".

Many might disagree with that grandiose statement but most would concede that the city is the music's spiritual birth-place.

Johnny Ace was a member of the seminal Beale Streeters vocal group in Memphis.

TEXAS

Big Blues from a Big State

RIGHT FROM THE EARLIEST DAYS OF THE MUSIC, TEXAN MUSICIANS HAVE PLAYED A MAJOR ROLE IN THE EVOLUTION OF THE BLUES. Not only has the Lone Star state's output of top bluesmen been prodigious, it has included some of the most charismatic and influential of them all. While they travelled far and wide to find their due acknowledgement—T-Bone Walker and Johnny "Guitar" Watson to Los Angeles, Freddie King to Chicago—they always carried the distinctive Chicago flavour with them.

Among the pioneers was the formidable Blind "Lemon" Jefferson, born in 1897 and a master of the acoustic blues, hammered out with ringing tones on a National steel guitar. Jefferson, who collapsed in the street from a heart attack and died of exposure in Chicago sometime around 1929, ended his life as penniless as he started out—but his legacy was formidable. He was truly as important for his influence on others as he was for his own sparse but magnificent recorded output, largely defining the musical framework of a whole generation of blues artists and even, many years later, inspiring the naming of the Jefferson Airplane rock band.

Better rewarded was Houston-based Sam "Lightnin'" Hopkins, who became an idol of the international folk-blues scene of the Sixties with his highly individual style. Much recorded, Hopkins was treated as a major star on the outdoor rock concert scene, as well as joining many of the blues packages which criss-crossed the US and Europe playing largely to white college audiences at a time when black youngsters had turned away from the blues to the more assertive "I'm black and I'm proud" soul music idiom of James Brown and his ilk. Hopkins studded his boots with beer bottle tops so he could beat out the rhythm in time with his rocking acoustic guitar work. Considering he spent most of his time living in big city Houston, it is amazing how downhome his music remained.

Though there were numerous

The long tall Texan—multi-talented Clarence "Gatemouth" Brown, without his stetson.

small labels active, Texan major league black music recording activity in the postwar years centred around the Duke/Peacock record labels, run by tough businessman Don Robey, who based his empire on the renowned Peacock Lounge where black music stars from all over America would come to play. Legend has it that Robey would prowl the ghetto streets, buying songs outright from down-at-heel young black songwriters for puny flat fees. These titles would eventually find their way on to wax with credits ascribed to the non-existent Deadric Malone.

Robey imported most of his artists from out-of-state—holding contracts on such major artists as Little Richard (pre the rock 'n' roll star's move to Specialty), Bobby "Blue" Bland, Johnny Ace and Little Junior Parker—but Clarence "Gatemouth" Brown was very much a home-grown talent, and he always wore a giant stetson to prove it!

Like Brown, other modern Texas artists have tended to show far more individuality than their counterparts from, say, Chicago. Albert Collins's style, for instance, has altered considerably over the years—from the clipped guitar phrasing of the "Frosty" period to the present ultra-high-volume histrionics which delight rock audiences around the world—while Johnny "Guitar" Watson, after starting out in a similar vein with incisive handfuls of notes displayed on his brilliant early hit 'Three Hours Past Midnight', moved into almost a psychedelic rock style when he became an international superstar.

Watson was just 13 years old when he moved from Houston to the West Coast, yet a strong Texan flavour always coloured his work and, like so many others, including the great B. B. King, he readily acknowledged the debt he owed to the masterful Aaron T-Bone Walker—surely one of the seminal figures across the whole spectrum of blues music.

Like many other leading black American musicians—Lowell Fulsom, Sugar Pie DeSanto and Chuck Berry included—Walker had part Red Indian blood coursing in his veins (in his case, Cherokee). His music was as distinctively individual as his personality and showed a strong jazz influence, picked up largely from listening to recordings by Charlie Christian.

Raised in Dallas, T-Bone taught himself to play guitar and learned early lessons in performing style by acting as guide to Blind Lemon Jefferson before touring with the Ida Cox Show and the Cab Calloway band. By 1934, he had moved to Los Angeles where he cut most of his formidable catalogue of recordings.

Blues critic Pete Welding described T-Bone Walker as "one of the most striking of all modern blues guitarists, possessing a matchless technique, impeccable taste and a flawless sense of rhythmic placement" while fellow Texan Freddie King summed up the man's towering influence when he told a *Melody Maker* interviewer in 1969: "I believe it all comes from T-Bone Walker. B. B. King and I were talking about that not long ago and he thinks so too."

THE WEST COAST

Go West Young Bluesman!

*T*HE TURBULENT YEARS FROM THE OUTBREAK OF THE SECOND WORLD WAR THROUGH TO THE FIFTIES WERE AN AGE OF MASSIVE MIGRATION FOR BLACK FAMILIES FROM THE POOR RURAL SOUTH TO THE INDUSTRIAL NORTH AND WEST, WHERE JOBS WERE RELATIVELY PLENTIFUL AND WELL PAID—PROVIDED YOU HAD THE REQUIRED MUSCLE POWER OR THE ABILITY TO HUSTLE.

While East Coasters tended to gravitate to New Jersey and New York and those from the Mississippi Delta and the Deep South to Chicago and Detroit, the burgeoning aircraft industry and busy shipyards of California provided an irresistible lure for itchy-footed blacks from Texas, Oklahoma and Kansas.

Lowell Fulsom (also spelt Fulson) was typical of the many musicians who took this route. Born in Tulsa, Oklahoma, he came from mixed stock, his father being a full-blood Cherokee Indian who played guitar while his mother and aunt were talented singers, dancers and guitarists.

In the late Thirties, Lowell had toured his home state with Texas Alexander, working the juke joints, before wartime naval service in the Pacific opened his eyes to a wider world. Returning to the USA, Lowell moved base to Oakland, California, where his hot combo, also featuring his brother Martin and, for a time, Ray Charles, became a popular club draw, recording for labels like Big Time, Swing Town and Aladdin. "It was an altogether more

Lowell Fulsom, a key figure in California's classy blues hierarchy.

lively scene, with lots of reasonably well paying work for a musician— but you had to be good to cut it," he recalls.

The Bay Area, around San Francisco, Berkeley and Oakland, and the rapidly growing metropolis of Los Angeles, boasted a plethora of labels. They provided a ready outlet for Fulsom and his peers—most of whom worked within a distinctive stylistic framework based on short, incisive guitar breaks, insistent riffs and fruity horn work.

Jimmy McCracklin, Lloyd Glenn, Percy Mayfield, Etta James, Johnny "Guitar" Watson, T-Bone Walker and many others worked the idiom—an intimate and restrained, yet intensely moody, form of R&B which bridged the gap between the blues and the all-pervasive soul music idiom which was fast gaining momentum locally through the pioneering recordings of Sam Cooke and others. Though much of Cooke's work, aimed at a mass white audience, veered towards pop, he also proved adept at interpreting the West Coast R&B idiom. Of all the many versions of Willie Dixon's 'Little Red Rooster' blues standard, Cooke's—which featured Billy Preston on organ and Ray Freeman on piano—was arguably the best.

For a time in the Fifties, touring package shows were all the rage. One of the last to survive—right into the late Seventies—was that led by the forceful Johnny Otis, who worked out of Los Angeles. A first-generation American of Greek parentage, Otis had a natural empathy for black musicians and black culture, as well as possessing a phenomenal ear for talent.

Etta James recalls how, as a 15-year-old, she was summoned with her two girlfriends to drop by Johnny's hotel for a late night audition. "We got this call saying he'd pay for the cab," she recalls. "He was out in the street waiting when we arrived at the hotel. I was so shy I had to go into the bathroom and close the door to sing, but he signed us up on the spot and next morning we were off on the road and within a few months 'Roll With Me Henry' was a big hit."

Another teenager, Little Esther Phillips—a little lady with a big blues ballad voice in the vein of Dinah Washington—was also a member of the Johnny Otis entourage, so too were Marie Adams and blues belter Big Mama Thornton.

Otis's Rhythm and Blues Caravan was to become a formidable nursery ground for West Coast blues artists—and provided steady employment for many talented sidemen.

Having produced hits by Johnny Ace and Little Richard for Duke/Peacock in earlier years, Otis was persuaded in 1974 to launch his own Blues Spectrum label.

Not that there had ever been any shortage of outlets for blues talent in that part of the world. Brothers Joe, Jules and Saul Bihari's Kent/ Modern/RPM set-up had a roster which included at various times Floyd Dixon, Smokey Hogg, Jimmy Witherspoon, Jimmy McCracklin, Etta James, B. B. King, Elmore James, Roscoe Gordon, Johnny "Guitar" Watson and Lowell Fulsom; Imperial headlined Jimmy McCracklin, T-Bone Walker, Smiley Lewis and Fats Domino; Art Rupe's Specialty boasted Roy Milton, Frankie Lee Sims, Percy Mayfield and Guitar Slim; Aladdin featured Amos Milburn, Charles Brown, Big Jay McNeely, Peppermint Harris, Lloyd Glenn and Floyd Dixon.

The locally produced product was almost always highly sophisticated, relying on superb musicianship, as well as feel, and aimed at a relatively cultured audience.

THE BLUES and SOUL CROSSOVER

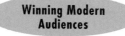

Winning Modern Audiences

*J*AZZ, BLUES, GOSPEL, SOUL, COUNTRY—THE CLASSIC AMERICAN MUSIC FORMS HAVE BETWEEN THEM SET THE GUIDELINES FOR POPULAR CULTURE AROUND THE WORLD. FROM THEIR HIGH ENERGY FUSION EMERGED FIRST ROCK 'N' ROLL AND THEN POP MUSIC AS WE KNOW IT TODAY.

These earlier patterns themselves grew from a multitude of influences—the tribal work songs and rhythmic patterns of America, the sea shanties learned from British sailors, the flavours of Europe, Asia, the Caribbean and the Latin world. And, despite the constraints of institutionalized segregation, there was always an intense interaction between the music of different American communities, black and white, big city or pastoral.

It is no surprise, then, that the borderlines between the various American music forms are so delightfully blurred. It's no real problem to music fans, who merely want to hear entertaining sounds, but it sure gives headaches to musicologists in their need to pigeon-hole everything. Do you file Ray Charles—to give just one instance—under jazz, blues, soul, gospel, pop, country, or whatever? After all, his music crosses many divides.

The advent of a more assertive new generation in the Sixties—young people who ascribed to the ideals of "I'm black and I'm proud" and who were demanding a new, better deal, as of right—saw the blues in danger of becoming an artistic backwater, a piece of history locked into a time-warp. Essentially inward-looking, reflective and often autobiographical, the blues usually told a story of hard times and bad luck, reflecting the earlier black experience but at odds with the brave new world of black self-assertiveness.

Mods in England might have packed the disco dance-floors to the sounds of John Lee Hooker's 'Boom Boom', but while older black Americans still enjoyed the hard-core blues, the younger generation had turned their backs on it, preferring the more forward-looking and often optimistic politicized themes or the pure and simple love stories which gave soul such massive appeal.

Audiences at blues concerts had become a sea of white student faces. In seeking to recapture its natural market among a native black American audience, it is no surprise

Like his namesake, Little Johnny Taylor, the talented Johnnie Taylor tinged his soul with a blues flavour.

that contemporary blues began adopting elements of soul.

It all started in the late Sixties when artists like Bobby "Blue" Bland, Little Milton, O. V. Wright, Little Johnny Taylor, Jimmy McCracklin, Ike Turner, Lowell Fulsom, Toussaint McCall, Robert Parker, Z. Z. Hill, Etta James and Sugar Pie DeSanto confidently straddled the divide between the two forms.

And soul stars returned the compliment. Sam Cooke cut a definitive version of Willie Dixon's 'Little Red Rooster', Otis Redding included a tremendous version of B. B. King's 'Rock Me Baby' on his seminal *Otis Blue* album and Al Green not only cut a powerhouse rendition of 'Driving Wheel'—a real vintage composition from Roosevelt Sykes—but also turned 'I Can't Get

Next To You', the Temptations' psychedelic soul opus, into a slab of pure gutbucket blues.

Booker T And The MGs, creators of the famed Memphis Soul Sound, backed Albert King on his blues albums for Stax and, on the other side of town, Willie Mitchell's team at Hi provided a similar framework for Jimmy McCracklin.

As the Sixties rolled into the Seventies and beyond, a generation of new, younger artists emerged who were ready and eager to exploit this blues and soul fusion. Typical of these was the harmonica-playing Little Sonny, an artist who, while undeniably tipping his cap to Sonny Boy Williamson, was as contemporary as you can get—and then some. Another was Bobby Rush, pictured on the sleeve of his début big-time album riding a sleek new BMW motorbike—a far cry from the broken-down shacks, moody sunsets and dusty roads which were the visual image of the blues past.

Others were seemingly even further removed from the originators. The big-voiced Latimore based himself in the unlikely location of Miami, Florida, dripped in jewellery, and never ever talked about having it tough, while Taj Mahal came from Ivy League territory in Massachusetts. This new music had little to do with two feet in the gutter: it breathed brash assertiveness.

Important new labels emerged to exploit the new dimension, notably Malaco, a company based in deepest Alabama but with its finger right on the pulse of modern trends. In a short time, Malaco gathered the talents of Bobby Bland, Little Milton, Z. Z. Hill, Johnnie Taylor and others to its bosom.

Into the Nineties, Ichiban emerged as another hot contender. Based just outside the fast-expanding city of Atlanta, Georgia, the company is headed up by former tour promoter, artist manager and founder of *Blues & Soul* magazine John E. Abbey, an Englishman who has spent a lifetime of involvement with black American music. "Soul grew out of the fusion of the blues with gospel so it is no wonder the crossover had always been so strong," he avers.

NEW ORLEANS
and the SWAMPS

Sound of
the Bayous

WHILE THE SAXOPHONE, KEYBOARDS, HARMONICA, BASS, DRUMS AND OTHER INSTRUMENTS ALL HAVE THEIR ROLE TO PLAY, IT IS THE GUITAR—WHETHER ACOUSTIC OR AMPLIFIED—WHICH HAS UNQUESTIONABLY BEEN THE DOMINANT INSTRUMENT IN BLUES MUSIC ACROSS AMERICA, EXCEPT, THAT IS, IN THE CRESCENT CITY OF NEW ORLEANS, WHERE THE PIANO HAS ALWAYS BEEN UNDISPUTED KING.

Whether this has happened by mere chance or, as seems more likely, because of the city's strong connection with French culture, is open to conjecture. Suffice to say that most of the music emanating from New Orleans has placed the piano (or sometimes the electric organ) in the lead role, whether it be the pounding rock 'n' roll cut in the city by Fats Domino, Little Richard and Larry Williams, the soul of Allen Toussaint and his artists like Lee Dorsey, Betty Harris and Ernie K. Doe, the funk of the Meters or the blues of Champion Jack Dupree, Professor Longhair, Roy Brown and Dr John.

Art Neville, leading light of the Neville Brothers family group which has itself run the gamut of soul to rock 'n' roll to jazz to blues and back again, believes that his native city pays little attention to musical divisions: "We all

play on each others' records and New Orleans' musicians, black and white alike, switch easily between different styles. But, whatever the music we are playing, there is a distinctive New Orleans' flavour to it and that usually entails a mass of exotic polyrhythms and not too strong an emphasis on solos."

As America's gateway to the Caribbean and a prime entry point for both goods and new immigrants from Europe, New Orleans has always had a distinctive atmosphere which distinguishes it from the North American norm. The famed French Quarter, though now largely taken over by tourists, is still a melting pot of flavours and a hotbed of great music—from the famous marching funeral bands to the quirky jazz and blues of the drinking dens.

The district nurtured Louis "Satchmo" Armstrong, the great jazz trumpeter, as its most famous son and also gave us the remarkable Champion Jack Dupree, a charismatic solo performer of mixed French, Red Indian and African-American descent who grew up in the same children's home and went on to evolve his own unique slant on the barrelhouse piano style which was so popular across the USA during the late Thirties.

Exceptions to the rule of piano dominance were Earl King and Snooks Eaglin. King played guitar in the strident fashion more usually associated with Chicago and those other three Kings, Albert, Freddie and B.B.—none of whom is related—while Eaglin's country blues-flavoured style has more in common with the music of the Mississippi Delta than with the big city.

Influences flowed into New Orleans not just from overseas but from the back country of the Louisiana swamplands, where voodoo and grisgris held sway and cajun, Creole and native Indian traditions all went into the melting-pot. It was there that the lively zydeco style, so entertainingly exploited by Clifton Chenier, Boozoo Chavis and others, evolved—with accordion replacing piano and the lyrics usually sung in Creole French, yet still very much part of the blues.

Record companies like Goldband in Lake Charles, Louisiana, Excello in Crowley, Louisiana, and Ace in Jackson, Mississippi, provided a ready outlet for out-of-town artists.

Run by amiable out-and-out music enthusiast Eddie Shuler—a man who usually put his joy for good-time sounds before any commercial considerations—Goldband was appropriately eclectic, giving a fascinating array of artists, from wild rockabillys and redneck "good old boy" country artists to down-home blues singers, the chance to put their talents on wax.

Shuler's son, Wayne, eventually landed a job as an A&R man with Capitol Records out in Hollywood. This move allowed the younger Shuler scope to introduce Louisiana's rising blues hope Guitar Junior (now known by his real name of Lonnie Brooks) to a wider audience. Baton Rouge's Neal brothers, Raful and Kenny, used the help of the Shulers and other local label-owners as a

King of the Louisiana swamp blues style—the much-missed Slim Harpo.

springboard to success. Ace's big names, notably Huey Piano Smith and Frankie Forde, veered in a novelty song direction with material which was more R&B than blues in form, but at Excello the sound was pure swamp blues.

Slim Harpo, with his whispering, Jimmy Reed-influenced voice and laid-back harmonica style, defined the magical Excello sound—a haunting and thoroughly original kind of music. Its other prime exponents included Lazy Lester, Silas Hogan and Lightnin' Slim.

COUNTRY BLUES

From the Fields and Back Porches

Left to right: Hammie Nixon, Sleepy John Estes and Yank Rachell—masters of acoustic country blues.

THE BLUES IS A PHENOMENON WHICH WAS ESSENTIALLY BORN WAY OUT IN THE REMOTE COUNTRY DISTRICTS OF THE SOUTHERN STATES BEFORE BEING CARRIED TO THE BIG CITIES AND NURTURED AS AMERICA'S GREATEST NATIVE ART FORM. WHILE MANY WILL ARGUE THAT IT WAS THE MISSISSIPPI DELTA WHICH GAVE BIRTH TO THIS UNIQUE MUSIC SOMETIME AROUND THE TURN OF THE CENTURY, THE TRUTH IS THAT IT PROBABLY SPRANG TO LIFE SPONTANEOUSLY IN A NUMBER OF DIFFERENT PLACES, ANYWHERE FROM THE CAROLINAS RIGHT THROUGH TO TEXAS.

Born out of the unaccompanied plantation-field hollers and spirituals of the rural poor, the blues also brought together more exotic influences.

Researching his vastly important *Southern Folk Heritage* series of recordings, released by Atlantic 30 years ago, Alan Lomax unearthed rhythmic traditions which could be traced straight back to the tribal music of West Africa, allied to melodies lifted out of eighteenth-century English folk music.

In remote rural communities, Lomax discovered primitive instruments like the cane fife and the mouth bow still filling a role long since passed to guitar and piano in more sophisticated towns and cities. Lonnie and Ed Young's eerie 'Hen Duck', as recorded by Lomax on a field trip through Virginia and the middle South to the Ozark Mountains and back to the Georgia Sea Islands in the summer of 1959, could almost as well have originated in darkest Africa, several thousand miles across the Atlantic.

Many older folk in country districts throughout the South remember music being made by the simple expedient of running a knife along a stretched piece of wire, its end wound around a nail fixed to the side of a wooden shack. Muddy Waters was just one of many stars-to-be who began making music in just this fashion. Washboards, one-string tea-chest basses and other do-it-yourself instruments all played a role before the arrival of a cheap mail-order guitar, usually bought after many months of saving.

While some musicians were also able to put the funding together to buy a cheap amplifier and then teamed up with like souls to form bands and work the cheap juke joints, others stayed faithful to the earlier, simpler, acoustic form. Some of these were even able to lift country blues from the back porch

to the folk festival and concert hall stage and make a veritable industry out of it.

The formidable Big Bill Broonzy, for instance, had already long since moved to big city Chicago and gone electric when he discovered in the Fifties that there was a whole new—and lucrative—young white student audience thirsting for the pure traditional form. To his delight, he saw that this following existed not only in America but in Europe too. Never one to miss a trick, he ditched his band and got rich.

By the Fifties, Brownie McGhee's brother Sticks was up in New York pumping out sophisticated uptown jump blues items like 'Drinking Wine Spo Dee O Dee' but guitarist Brownie and his blind harmonica-playing partner Sonny Terry, who had first teamed up to play minstrel shows across North Carolina in 1939, stuck to the acoustic form to find a mass international audience for their slant on the country blues.

Other artists like Leadbelly (Huddie Ledbetter), Josh White, Big Joe Williams, Skip James, Sleepy John Estes and Mississippi Fred McDowell mined a similarly rich vein, skilfully surrounding themselves with a mystique and an exotic charisma which middle-class city kids found irresistible. Leadbelly, for example, fully exploited the myths and legends which interwove the truth of his colourful life—and encouraged the story of his nickname having been derived from his stomach being peppered full of buckshot.

Born on a plantation near Mooringsport, Louisiana, in 1899, Leadbelly hoboed across the Southern States in his youth, running into trouble with the law and serving time in Shaw State Prison for homicide. Recordings for the Library of Congress between 1934 and 1938 won him a following sufficient to warrant a move to New York City, where he worked the local parties, folk lofts and political rallies, eventually linking up with Sonny Terry, Brownie McGhee and white folk singer Woody Guthrie as the darling of the Greenwich Village hootenanny scene and appearing on television and in movies through to his death in 1949.

For some country artists, such wider recognition came too late to bring them any personal fortune—though their names are indelibly inscribed in the blues Hall of Fame. Blind Willie McTell, who also worked under such aliases as Hot Shot Willie, Blind Doogie and Pig 'n' Whistle Red; "Memphis Blues Boy" Willie Nix, who started out as a tap dancer with the Rabbit Foot Minstrels Show; Revd Blind Gary Davis, unusual in being a preacher who played "the Devil's Music";

B. B. King's cousin, Bukka White; Stackhouse Houston, who played guitar, harmonica, violin and mandolin; Hammie Nixon, who fathered 16 children, and others had all continued a tradition started by such pre-war greats as Blind Blake, Scrapper Blackwell, Yank Rachell, Railroad Bill and Blind Willie Walker—many of whose lives were shrouded in mystery, their ethereal voices reaching out across the years to us via scratchy but still intensely powerful 78-rpm recordings.

Some fine traditional country blues is still to be heard—the white artist John Hammond Jr. being a particularly fine exponent—but it is essentially a music belonging to a long past age, its development probably arrested as long ago as the early 1930s when, as respected blues critic Samuel B. Charters put it in his book *The Country Blues*: "Leroy Carr almost completely changed the style of popular blues singing. He was a city man, playing piano, and his singing was much less intense than that of the country bluesmen who had gone before him."

CAN WHITE MEN SING the BLUES ?

The Rock 'n' Roll Crossover

CREATED OUT OF THE MISERY AND DEPRIVATION OF THE RURAL SOUTH, HONED IN THE BRUTAL GHETTOS OF THE INDUSTRIAL NORTH, THE BLUES HAVE BEEN THE REMARKABLE CHRONICLE OF THE BLACK AMERICAN EXPERIENCE. YET, RIGHT FROM THE EARLY DAYS, WHITES—AND NOT JUST AMERICANS EITHER—HAVE HAD THEIR ROLE TO PLAY IN THE MUSIC'S DEVELOPMENT.

It was, for many years, almost exclusively, white-owned record labels which gave the blues its commercial outlet. The big companies like Columbia, Decca and RCA were not, of course, involved for altruistic reasons—they saw black music as a strong source of sales and, given the low overheads involved, with artist fees usually consisting of a flat fee set at a derisory level, they knew that profit margins could be high. They launched special labels dedicated to what they called "race music" and blacks rushed to buy whatever appeared under the OKeh (Columbia), Vocalion (Decca) and Bluebird (RCA) logos.

By the late Thirties, there was even a nascent if still limited white audience for the blues, as proved by the success of John Hammond Snr's pioneering *Spirituals To Swing* concerts at Carnegie Hall. Legend has it that "King

White harmonica player Paul Butterfield grew up in the blues-rich Chicago urban environment.

of the Delta Bluesmen" Robert Johnson's contract to appear on Hammond's bill was posted to him on the very day that the emergent star was murdered.

The BMI copyright agency was founded in order to break the big song publishers' monopoly and the resulting emergence of a rash of small independent labels—some, by now, owned by blacks—broke the blues scene wide open during the immediate post-war years. Despite

27

the changes, however, the business end of affairs continued to be dominated by Caucasians but now they were taking more than a mere money-counting interest and were also getting involved with creating the music, not just as songwriters and record producers but as studio musicians too.

Then came the Sixties, the folk-music revolution headed by Bob Dylan and the beat explosion led by the Beatles. Rock 'n' roll had already changed everything. Whites were not only involved with making money out of black music—now, ever-increasing numbers of them wanted to listen to it too.

Bigoted Bible Belt fire-and-brimstone preachers might have ranted about the evil influence of what they disparagingly called "nigger music" but kids knew what they wanted to hear and, soon, many of them wanted to play it as well.

Dylan unashamedly dipped into the blues songbook—and even recorded some obscure country blues items, masquerading as the mythical Blind Boy Grunt—while the Beatles, the Rolling Stones and others were swift to give credit to the black performers who were their prime inspiration.

Blues purists—few of whom were themselves black—were outraged that white musicians—some of them British, at that—should imitate their revered black American idols. Black America, on the other hand, graciously accepted imitation as the sincerest form of flattery and shrugged shoulders at the raging controversy over "can white men sing the blues?" Today, few would deny that the answer is "yes"—the argument having been deflated for the fraud it is when an astute music journalist posed the question "can blue men sing the whites?"

It was in the folk blues idiom that white artists first made their mark with recordings that could be taken seriously. The Greenwich Village folk scene in New York and the pioneering Elektra label provided us with powerful white blues from the likes of Spider John Koerner, Dave "Snakey" Ray, Dave Van Ronk, Tom Rush and John Hammond Jr.

The late Stevie Ray Vaughn was an authentic white blues talent.

But it was in Europe that the first credible white electric blues bands emerged, the movement being spearheaded by the remarkably talented harmonica player Cyril Davies—who sadly died before the music emerged from underground status—and his partner Alexis Korner. It was from the duo's "All Stars" that talents like Long John Baldry and the nucleus of the Rolling Stones emerged. The whole R&B and beat group movement had, indeed, been rooted in the skiffle music of a few years earlier when artists like Lonnie Donegan gave a new slant to blues songs learned from rare imported records by Leadbelly and Big Bill Broonzy.

The trickle quickly became a flood. Tyneside's Animals tore into a range of blues classics, Van Morrison and Them emerged from Belfast to repeat the old Big Joe Williams's plea 'Baby Please Don't Go', and John Mayall's Bluesbreakers provided the outfit from which Eric "Slowhand" Clapton emerged to become, arguably, the greatest white exponent of the blues.

Nor was white America about to be outdone by the Brits. From Chicago came the blues-wailing Paul Butterfield Band, featuring Elvin Bishop and Mike Bloomfield. Ry Cooder, J. J. Cale and the late, great, Stevie Ray Vaughn showed the white slant on the blues need not be wholly derivative, while Janis Joplin passed into legend and harmonica wizard Charlie Musselwhite became a cult figure, earning the respect of black and white musicians and fans alike.

What's more, such major black bluesmen as B. B. King, Albert King, Earl Hooker and Buddy Guy increasingly employed white musicians for both studio and stage work and, in more recent times, Bonnie Raitt brought her brilliant guitar work and vocals into play on John Lee Hooker's best-selling remake of 'In The Mood'. Robert Cray is well-known for employing a white backing band.

Back in the late Sixties, R&B enthusiast Mike Vernon left Decca to set up his own Blue Horizon label, providing a framework from which Fleetwood Mac was able to graduate from the blues to a role as the biggest selling rock band of all time. To this day, in clubs around the world, aspiring blues bands, many with no desire to achieve anything other than enjoy playing the music they love, belt out their own versions of the classics.

WOMEN in the BLUES

The Ladies Sing the Blues

*T*HOUGH THE BLUES HAS BEEN, TO A VERY LARGE DEGREE, A MALE-DOMINATED ART-FORM, WOMEN HAVE PLAYED AN HONOURED ROLE IN ITS DEVELOPMENT—NOT JUST IN PROVIDING THE THEMES FOR SO MANY OF ITS GREAT SONGS BUT AS PERFORMERS TOO.

Given the rabid prejudices of the time—against blacks in general, against women and against blues music as an idiom—it took an especially tough kind of lady to make her career in the blues during the early years of the music's development and the lives of so many of the pioneers were tinged with tragedy.

Everyone knows the story of Billie Holiday—distorted, maybe, from seeing the over-romanticized *The Lady Sings The Blues*, starring Diana Ross, but correct in its essence. The prejudice she met out on the road, her broken romances, her spine-chilling rendition of 'Strange Fruit', a haunting song about a lynching, with lyrics by poet Lewis Allen, and her drug addiction and eventual death from an overdose while detained in New York's Metropolitan Hospital awaiting charges for possession are all stark truth.

It was an experience mirrored in the lives of other ladies of the blues. Bessie Smith, the greatest of them all, died of shock and blood loss after being refused admission to a whites-only hospital following a car accident near Coahama, Mississippi, while Ida Cox found her steps dogged by female impersonator Sam Fouche, who aped Ida's stage billing as "the Sepia Mae West",

and the songs of Victoria Spivey reflected just how tough it could be. As Jim O'Neal put it in *Rolling Stone* magazine: "Many of her blues were grim tales of death, despair, cruelty and agony, underscored by her sombre piano and stark Texas blues moan."

Justifiably tagged as "the Empress of the Blues", Bessie Smith was one of four unrelated Smiths who made a major impact on the distaff side of the music in the pre-war years. South Carolina-born Clara Smith had a voice tinged with such melancholy it could chill the warmest blood. Trixie Smith, born in Atlanta in 1895, was one of the earliest of the vaudeville-style blues artists to record, and Mamie Smith, born in Cincinnati sometime around May 26, 1883, was said by blues researcher Paul Oliver to have, through her pioneering work, "paved the way for every other blues artist to come, regardless of style".

Other names reach out across the years, including the great Ma Rainey, to many the best of them all—though, such was the depth of her talent that she often departed from the blues into jazz and bawdy vaudeville songs.

The prolific Ethel Waters, who brought the blues to London as early as 1929, Creole artist Lizzie Miles, the unrelated Josephine Miles, ragtime pianist Ada Brown, Memphis Minnie, Hattie McDaniel, Viola McCoy and others played a role in the early development of the blues, most of them displaying a far higher degree of sophistication than their male counterparts.

New names emerged after the Second World War. Dinah Washington, a real tough lady who was given to beating up her errant husband on stage, was among the best though she, like many of her predecessors, often strayed from the blues into jazz territory. That path was also followed by the redoubtable Nina Simone, a lady whose eventful life saw her know at first hand almost the entire gamut of the blues experience. She was lover to chauffeurs and millionaires, to African politicians and French gigolos, raised a child on her own,

went from rags to riches and back again, experienced racism at its most vitriolic and became a leading light of the civil rights movement. Her atmospheric *Nina Simone Sings The Blues* album, with its chilling themes, is arguably one of the great blues recordings of all time.

West Coasters Little Esther Phillips and Etta James, both protégées of bandleader Johnny Otis, brought the soul and blues styles into total harmony with their many superb recordings, Etta's sterling work continuing to this day. The Chess company, for which Etta cut her very best work, was also home for KoKo Taylor and Sugar Pie DeSanto. Sugar Pie is now semi-retired, working as an office clerk in California, but KoKo continues to belt out the blues and record regularly. Another formidable talent is Big Mama Thornton, the originator of 'Hound Dog'.

The piano has been the chosen instrument of most female blues artists and one of its best current exponents is Louisiana's Katie Webster, a powerhouse lady who

Long-serving Chicago songstress Koko Taylor represents the distaff side of blues at its best.

has taken her brand of barrelhouse boogie-woogie to audiences across the globe.

Texas gives us the big voice of Trudy Lynn, who now records for Ichiban in Atlanta. Another name to look for is Gwen McCrae, whose deep soul style veers ever closer to pure blues. Nor should we overlook the contribution of white blues artists Janis Joplin and Bonnie Raitt, both in the Who's Who section.

THE BLUES KALEIDOSCOPE

A Music of Many Facets

THE BLUES, LIKE LOVE, IS A MANY-SPLENDOURED THING. THE CLASSIC 12-BAR FORMAT, RATHER THAN BEING OPPRESSIVELY CONSTRICTIVE, ALLOWS FOR MANY VARIATIONS ON A THEME. BESIDES THE VARIOUS REGIONAL BLUES STYLES—USUALLY SHAPED BY THE NATURE OF THE PARTICULAR COMMUNITIES WHICH GAVE THEM BIRTH— THERE ARE WIDER DIVISIONS WITHIN THE MUSIC.

The honking big band blues which started from Kansas City and rapidly spread nationwide, the screaming electric blues of guitar/bass/drums format, the classic ragtime, barrelhouse and boogie-woogie piano styles—all provided wide dimension and an ever-changing kaleidoscope of sound.

As the nation's prime metropolis, New York had no real need to develop a blues style of its own, for musicians from every corner of the country beat a path there, to record, to play the clubs and concert halls, to find fame.

Founded by brothers Nesuhi and Ahmed Ertegun, the jazz-loving sons of a Turkish ambassador to the USA, and their original partner Herb Abramson, Atlantic Records quickly established itself as one of the greatest black music labels of all, taking Ray Charles to superstardom and packaging the music of other, often more esoteric, artists for mass consumption.

Sue Records sneaked some blues in among the R&B and Bobby Robinson's Fire and Fury labels brought us the wild bottleneck sound of Elmore James.

Across the Hudson River in Newark, New Jersey, labels like Savoy (with Nappy Brown, Big Jay McNeely, Big Maybelle, Wilbert Harrison and others) and the Milestone/Prestige group (King Curtis, John Lee Hooker and so many more) also showcased blues.

Fittingly for a big, brash city, the blues shouters always did well in the Big Apple. Huge barrel-chested men, with equally big voices, stars like Big Joe Turner, Jimmy Witherspoon, Joe Williams and Jimmy Rushing were regular headliners at Harlem's near-legendary Apollo Theatre, along with such locally based female blues-slanted stars as Ruth Brown, LaVern Baker and Big Maybelle.

Fittingly for men who had honed their style in Kansas City, the home town of bebop jazz's key figure,

Charlie "Yardbird" Parker, the great blues shouters were as much at home in front of the jazz big bands of Jay McShann, Count Basie and Duke Ellington as they were when working with small combos.

Jazzmen regularly included blues themes in their repertoire and many musicians were equally at home in either music. Sax maestros like King Curtis, Louis Jordan, Tiny Bradshaw, Ben "Bull Moose" Jackson, Red Prysock and Big Jay McNeely favoured the blues idiom, but they all cut straight jazz records too.

The blues pianists also covered plenty of ground. From the early, unsophisticated days of players like Cow Cow Davenport, Meade Lux Lewis, Speckled Red and his brother Dr Feelgood, who played 'The Dirty Dozens' in bordellos and illicit drinking dens, emerged a wide diversity of styles of varying degrees of sophistication.

In the Thirties, Frankie "Half Pint" Jaxon was one of the first to break into the theatres and on to radio while two decades later the emergent Ray Charles, who also played mean saxophone, based his sophisticated piano-playing on the work of Charles Brown, Lloyd Glenn and Nat King Cole.

In contrast, the brash, slick Willie Mabon used his polished piano style to frame sexually suggestive *double entendre* lyrics and, at the other end of the spectrum, Otis Spann's sound was still rooted in the raw Mississippi Delta style. Smiley Lewis, like his contemporary, Fats Domino, framed his vocals with the distinctive and often simplistic couplets of the New Orleans tradition, and Louisiana-born and well-travelled Little Brother Montgomery provided a poignant link back to an earlier era.

Harmonica players also often took a leading role, though in a less diverse range of styles. Sonny Boy Williamson I (John Lee Williamson) lost his life, stabbed to death with an ice pick, in 1947 but he had set the scene for a whole generation of Chicago mouth harp players. The cudgel was taken up by such greats as Little Walter, Walter "Shakey" Horton, Junior Wells, James Cotton, John Brim, Jimmy Reed and, the giant of them all, Sonny Boy Williamson II, alias Rice Miller.

Willie Nix and Roy Milton, washboard exponents Washboard Willie and George "Papa" Lightfoot, bassist Willie Dixon and kazoo player Gus Cannon all got to front their own records. As for Jessie "Lone Cat" Fuller and Wilbert Harrison—they were full-blown one-man bands in their own right!

A bass player who led his own band—the formidable Willie Dixon wrote many of the classic blues songs.

JOHNNY ACE

When a gunshot rang out backstage at the City Auditorium in Houston on Christmas Eve 1954 it signalled the tragically abrupt end to the career of one of black music's brightest shooting stars.

A sometime member of the seminal Beale Streeters group in Memphis—along with Bobby Bland and Roscoe Gordon—Johnny Ace was born in that city on June 9, 1929, his real name being John Marshall Alexander Jr. Signed to Duke Records by Don Robey, the 23-year-old topped the R&B chart in 1952 with his début record, 'My Song'. Ace toured as a double-header with Big Mama Thornton and soon became a major attraction, earning acclaim by *Cashbox* magazine as "The most programmed R&B artist of 1954". Thanks to his warm baritone and an urbane style which was in many ways a progenitor of the soon to emerge soul music idiom, Ace seemed in line for a superstar career but blew his brains out playing Russian roulette for a handful of dollars. His biggest hit, the classic blues ballad 'Pledging My Love' was released posthumously.

LUTHER ALLISON

Cited as one of the most original exponents of the modern electric blues idiom, Luther Allison effectively updated the sound of players like Albert King, Buddy Guy, Otis Rush and Magic Sam and earned the added distinction of actually recording for Motown for a time—though without in any way compromising his hard-belting and intensely emotive creativity. He also at one time was a member of the Rolling Stones—not, however, the British rock band but a

Chicago outfit of that name which he formed with his brother Grant in 1957 after moving north from Arkansas (where he had been born in rural Mayflower on August 17, 1939) and initially playing in the band of another brother, Ollie Lee Allison.

After stints with Jimmy Dawkins, Freddie King, Magic Sam and others, Luther spent much of 1968 working in Los Angeles with Shakey Jake and recorded there for World Pacific. Returning to Chicago, he became a fixture on the local club scene as well as touring throughout the Midwest and Canada, making numerous fine albums for a range of labels and appearing on the soundtrack for the Motown-backed movie *Cooley High*. By the late Seventies, he had also become a regular visitor to Europe.

LaVern Baker

Straddling the straight blues and commercial R&B styles, and paving the way towards soul music, LaVern Baker was a giant of the American black music scene during her stint with Atlantic Records, from 1952 to 1965, though the last half-decade had seen interest tail off as attention swung to more modern styles. Her updating of the traditional 'See See Rider' was a prime example of the way in which Atlantic worked the blues vein, giving it polish and making it a flawless gem in their formidable musical crown.

Born in Chicago on November 11, 1929, LaVern was one of the first R&B artists to attract a big following with white audiences.

The electrifying Luther Allison makes his guitar cry the blues.

Carey Bell

Though soaking up the influences of Sonny Boy Williamson, Walter "Shakey" Horton, Sonny Terry and other mouth harp players, Chicago-based Carey Bell has essentially been his own man—"His harmonica modulations and nuances are all of his own development—almost harpsichordic in effect and a really refreshing innovative aural experience", as music writer Len Kunstadt put it.

A native of Macon, Mississippi, where he was born on November 14, 1936, Carey taught himself harmonica at the age of 8 and later became proficient on drums, guitar and bass as well. Running away from home, he worked outside music before joining his stepfather Lovey Lee's country and western band, first in Mississippi then, from 1956, in Chicago. He soon became part of the local blues scene, sitting in with Big Walter, Johnny Young, Eddie Taylor and others before joining Earl Hooker's touring band in 1968 and making his own recording début for Delmark.

After first visiting Europe as a member of John Lee Hooker's band in 1969, he made numerous return trips, working with Jimmy "Fastfingers" Dawkins, Muddy Waters and others. Regular releases on Alligator, BluesWay, Rounder, Flying Fish and other labels have kept his name prominent.

SCRAPPER BLACKWELL

Guitarist Scrapper Blackwell's Twenties and Thirties recordings with pianist Leroy Carr shine down through the years as true landmarks in the development of the blues. They ushered in an altogether more sophisticated approach, for the time, than that of the down home musicians who had given birth to the music.

Born in the Carolinas, on February 21, 1903, Scrapper, whose mother was of Red Indian descent, had moved to Indianapolis when he was just six. Self-taught, he played guitar at parties around Indianapolis and Chicago before teaming with Leroy Carr in 1928 and recording for Vocalion, Bluebird and Champion-Decca.

After Carr's early death in 1935, at the age of 30, from alcohol-induced nephritis, Scrapper went into semi-retirement—though working occasional party, tavern, lounge and concert dates as a solo. He returned to recording, for 77 Records, in 1959 and cut an album for Prestige-Bluesville in 1961 but on October 7, 1962, he was shot dead in an Indianapolis back alley.

From ghetto backyard to recording stardom—Scrapper Blackwell brought urban sophistication to the blues scene.

BOBBY BLAND

See separate entry in the Legends section.

MIKE BLOOMFIELD

The quicksilver-fingered Mike Bloomfield was one of an élite coterie of young white musicians who hung out in the Southside Chicago blues clubs of the Sixties, picking up the influence of Muddy Waters, Buddy Guy, Otis Rush and others.

Born in Chicago in 1943, Mike made his reputation with the hard-hitting Paul Butterfield Blues Band. Under the guidance of Bob Dylan's charismatic manager Albert Grossman, he joined the potent black drummer Buddy Miles to form Electric Flag as a short-lived but brilliantly innovative band which married the blues and rock idioms. The success of the *Super Session* album, on which Mike Bloomfield co-starred with Stephen Stills and Al Kooper, was not matched by a further trio outing on which he shared the honours with white bluesmen John Paul Hammond and Dr John. However, his 1977 'If You Love These Blues Please Play Them', on which he replicated the styles of the great blues masters, served as a primer for thousands of aspiring young players.

Another casualty of rock 'n' roll, he died on February 14, 1981, at the early age of 38, leaving behind a legacy of potent music.

LONNIE BROOKS (AKA GUITAR JUNIOR)

One of the younger generation of Chicago blues greats, Lonnie Brooks began his career in the Deep South, being discovered by Eddie Shuler, boss of Goldband Records (based in Lake Charles, Louisiana) in 1957.

Born on December 18, 1933, in Dubuisson, Louisiana, he was raised first in nearby Garland, then in Port Arthur Texas, and learned music from his banjo-playing grandfather. Early experience in the cajun band of Clifton Chenier and his first recordings led to a move to Chicago where Lonnie worked with Jimmy Reed's band and played on numerous blues/R&B/soul sessions through the Sixties, as well as recording in his own right for One-Der-Ful, USA, Palos, Chess and, under the aegis of Shuler's son, Wayne, for Capitol, using his pseudonym of Guitar Junior.

By the mid-Seventies, his fame had spread further afield and Lonnie toured with the Chicago Blues Festival package throughout Europe and recorded regularly for Alligator. He should not be confused with Luther Johnson Jr. who also used the Guitar Jr. alias.

BIG BILL BROONZY

See separate entry in the Legends section.

CHARLES BROWN

Charles Brown was one of the most influential of all the talented artists in the West Coast "cool" school of blues/R&B—Ray Charles, Fats Domino, Amos Milburn and others borrowing elements of his sophisticated vocal and keyboard styles.

He was born in 1920 and grew up in Texas City, just outside Galveston, Texas. Arriving in California in 1943, he worked as an elevator operator before winning a talent contest, not with a blues but with 'Clair de Lune'. Following a stint as pianist with bandleader Bardu Ali, Charles joined Johnny Moore and Ed Williams to form the Three Blazers, one of the R&B scene's most successful acts, cutting numerous songs which went on to become blues standards. The first session for Aladdin yielded the smash hit 'Driftin' Blues', which Charles had written when just 12 years old.

Stints with Modern and Exclusive—including the 1949 classic 'Merry Christmas Baby', since covered by James Brown, Chuck Berry, Elvis Presley and many others—and a return to Aladdin produced a consistent run of Three Blazers hits.

Charles worked as a solo through the Fifties and toured the South with Johnny Ace as the hottest package in the land in 1954. He continued to record and tour prolifically through to present times, but with a far lower profile. His work is still widely appreciated, however, especially by other musicians

Charles Brown drifted from Texas to California to become a leader of the "cool" school of blues.

CLARENCE "GATEMOUTH" BROWN

Exuberant and ever smiling, Clarence "Gatemouth" Brown is one of the most enigmatic of all bluesmen, able to change direction and mood like the wind. He started out as a drummer, became one of the most influential electric guitarists of the Texas blues school then turned the violin into an authentic deep blues instrument. Schooled in blues he also had a feeling for country and western music, always sporting a stetson and on one notable occasion recording with Nashville giant Roy Clark.

Raised on his father's ranch at Orange, Texas, Gatemouth was born on April 18, 1924, in Vinton, Louisiana, and learned music at home, his father playing regularly in local bands.

After playing drums with William Benbow's Brownskin Models through the Midwest in the early Forties, he joined the Hart Hughes Orchestra working out of San Antonio.

Gatemouth's first recordings, in 1947, were cut for Aladdin Records in Los Angeles, with the Maxwell Davis Orchestra. He also worked as a resident act at Don Robey's Bronze Peacock Club in Houston and recorded for the Peacock label, as well as touring in the early Fifties with labelmate Big Mama Thornton.

The Chicago Blues Festival brought him to Europe in 1971 and Gatemouth made many return visits, becoming especially popular in France. He still found time to work outside music as deputy sheriff of San Juan County in New Mexico, his home since the early Sixties, at which time he doubled up as a country and western singer with regular Nashville club appearances.

His prolific recording schedule and work for the US State Department throughout Africa further strengthened Gatemouth's deservedly strong international following.

ROY BROWN

Along with Ray Charles and Sam Cooke, New Orleans' stylish Roy Brown was one of the fathers of soul music while rating recognition as a blues shouter extraordinary. Like most big-name Crescent City artists, Roy favoured piano rather than guitar as his instrument. Born on September 10, 1925, he was schooled in gospel music and formed the Rookie Four gospel quartet in his home city before moving to Los Angeles in 1942 to work as a professional boxer. After winning numerous talent shows, he opted for a musical career and moved to Galveston, Texas, to form the Melodeers, work as a duo—the Blues Twins—with Clarence Samuels, and record as a solo for Gold Star.

By the early Fifties, his records for De Luxe and King were beginning to have national impact.

During the Sixties, Roy recorded for a variety of labels, worked regularly with the Johnny Otis Revue, and visited Britain in 1978. He died on May 25, 1981, in San Fernando, California.

PAUL BUTTERFIELD

White musician Paul Butterfield learned his harmonica-playing craft from such greats as Little Walter, Walter "Shakey" Horton, James Cotton and Junior Wells in the Southside blues clubs of Chicago, the city where he had been born on December 17, 1942.

In the mid-Sixties he pulled in drummer Sam Lay, bassist Jerome Arnold, who had lately been with Howlin' Wolf's band, and guitarist Smokey Smothers to form his first band. Replacing Smothers with Elvin Bishop and then drafting in another young white guitarist, Mike Bloomfield, he created the classic line-up of the Paul Butterfield Blues Band, which cut exuberant electric blues albums for Elektra from 1965. The inventive instrumental title track from *East-West* married the blues to an Indian raga scale, creating a whole new musical direction.

Paul Butterfield also cut an EP with John Mayall, featuring Peter Green on guitar, and was a guest on Muddy Waters's *Father And Sons* double album, a project which reunited him with Bloomfield, who had earlier left for solo stardom. In later years, Paul played on white girl blues singer Bonnie Raitt's first efforts.

Black bluesman Mojo Bufford rated Paul Butterfield as "the best harmonica player today—black or white."

A true colossus of the black music world, Ray Charles well merits his tag of "the Genius".

RAY CHARLES

Dubbed—not unjustifiably—"the Genius", Ray Charles is a true giant of American music, his 45-year career having straddled the blues, soul, jazz, country and western and pop music divides.

Born in Albany, Georgia, on September 23, 1930, his full name was Ray Charles Robinson, his surname being dropped to avoid confusion with the boxer Sugar Ray Robinson. Permanently blinded at the age of 6, Ray was raised at a state school for the blind in Florida and by his late teens had become a full-time musician, working in Jacksonville and Orlando before moving to Seattle, where he joined bluesman Lowell Fulsom's band. He then formed a trio, led by his own piano playing and vocals and loosely based on the music of the Nat "King" Cole trio and influential West Coast blues paragon Charles Brown, and recorded for local labels.

Ray's career took off in earnest when the Ertegun brothers signed him to Atlantic Records in 1952. Many of his early records for them were in a solid blues mood, including the up-tempo 12-bar opus 'Mess Around' and the hypnotic 'Lonely Avenue'.

Having already defined the direction of the emergent soul music idiom, Ray moved even further from the blues in 1962 with the milestone *Modern Sounds In Country & Western*. This opened up a huge popular audience for "Uncle Ray", as he was by then affectionately known in black music circles.

CLIFTON CHENIER

Clifton Chenier's distinctive music was born in the Cajun swamp country of rural Louisiana and was strongly flavoured by the folk tradition of the Acadians (French settlers who had moved south *en masse* when Britain took over Canada). Instruments like the fiddle and the accordion were highly popular and it was the latter which Clifton adopted to become the foremost exponent of the black Louisiana blues/Cajun hybrid known as zydeco, a style which often incorporates lyrics in patois French.

In his teens, Clifton worked on farms outside Opelousas, where he had been born on June 25, 1925. Along with his washboard-playing brother Cleveland, Clifton worked in the Clarence Garlow band before forming his own outfit and working as far afield as Los Angeles where, in 1955, he recorded for Specialty.

He moved to Houston in 1958 and many other labels, including Argo, Checker, Zynn, Arhoolie and Crazy Cajun issued his records. In 1967 he visited Europe for the first time, appearing at the Royal Albert Hall. His uncle, Morris Chenier, was also a popular zydeco artist.

ERIC CLAPTON

Though his music has since strayed far from the confines of the blues, Eric "Slowhand" Clapton was, in his day, arguably the finest white exponent of the style.

Born in middle-class suburbia at Ripley, Surrey, he was brought up by foster parents and attended Kingston Art College, where he was exposed to the records of Muddy Waters, Big Bill Broonzy, Howlin' Wolf and other greats and taught himself to play guitar.

In 1963, Eric formed the Roosters, a seminal outfit which at various times included Paul Jones and Mike McGuinness of the Manfred Mann group and Rolling Stones founder member Brian Jones. Later that year Eric spent a fortnight with Casey Jones and the Engineers before replacing Tony "Top" Topham as lead guitarist with the newly formed Yardbirds. The band quickly built a fanatical following and recorded with Sonny Boy Williamson, but differences over a change of musical direction led the then purist Eric Clapton to quit for a post with John Mayall's Bluesbreakers, a straight-ahead Chicago blues style outfit.

Eric's time with the Mayall band helped build a cult status which led to the graffitied legend "Clapton is God" appearing on walls all over London. Since those heady days, Eric has moved into the rock mainstream.

Fans once proclaimed "Clapton is God". Truth is, he has been one of the best white exponents of blues music.

43

ALBERT COLLINS

Albert Collins's quick-fire staccatto guitar approach, with its spare, clipped phrasing, was one of the most distinctive sounds in Sixties R&B, giving him a run of minor hits with such cool instrumentals as 'Frosty'. Since then, his style has become closer in form to that of B. B. King—and much more brash too—with drawn-out notes, heavy use of vibrato and a surfeit of volume. These days, he sings a lot more too.

The man cited by many as the best of the Texas guitarists was born on a farm at Leona, Texas, on October 3, 1932, moving to big city Houston as a youngster. Work in local clubs led to early recording dates for Kangaroo, Great Scott and Hall from 1958 on. By the mid-Sixties, Albert had a nationwide reputation, bringing him deals with 20th Century, Imperial and others and bookings on major blues festivals, including visits to Europe. Twenty-five years on, he remains a major draw.

Albert is a cousin of Lightnin' Hopkins.

JAMES COTTON

It was hearing Sonny Boy Williamson II (Rice Miller) on local radio that inspired the then 7-year-old James Cotton to take up harmonica playing. He ran away from home in 1944, when he was 9, to learn more of the art at the feet of the master, working with Sonny Boy, Willie Nix, Howlin' Wolf and others in the clubs and being allowed to make the occasional appearance on Sonny Boy's *King Biscuit Time* radio show. When Williamson moved his base to Chicago, James took over his mentor's band and cut his début records.

Muddy Waters passed through Memphis in 1954 and invited James to join his band, a role which the young player filled off-and-on until 1966. By the mid-Sixties, James was enjoying the limelight in his own right, cutting a number of fine albums.

Renowned for his energetic live appearances, James, who was born in Tunica, Mississippi, on July 1, 1935, remains a major figure to this day.

IDA COX

Billed as "the Sepia Mae West", the charismatic Ida Cox was among the greatest of all the classic blues singers. As a 14-year-old she ran away from home to work with the White And Clark Black And Tan Minstrels, having developed an interest in music from singing in the African Methodist Church choir at Cedartown, Georgia, where her family had settled shortly after her birth on February 25, 1896 in Tacoa, Georgia.

She moved on to the better-known Rabbit Foot Minstrels and changed her name from Ida Prather to Ida Cox—though she was also known, at various times, as Velma Bradley, Kate Lewis, Julia Powers and Jane Smith! Work with Jelly Roll Morton in the early Twenties led to a contract with Paramount for whom she recorded prolifically in Chicago and New York.

'Ida's own Darktown Scandals Review worked theatres across America through the Thirties and she toured with old friend Billie Pierce in the early Forties but soon entered semi-retirement, re-emerging in 1961 to record in New York for Riverside, accompanied by the redoubtable jazz sax player Coleman Hawkins. She died of cancer on November 10, 1967, in Knoxville, Tennessee, where she had made her home since 1949.

ROBERT CRAY

Undoubtedly the most important, and commercially successful, of the new generation blues players, Robert Cray has helped assure the music's future and its continued development, thanks to his inventive approach. Robert's 1986 *Strong Persuader* was the first pure blues album to hit the upper reaches of the American album charts in 15 years and paved the way for the rebirth of John Lee Hooker's fortunes.

Son of a soldier, Robert was born at Fort Benning, Georgia, on August 1, 1953, and grew up in Eugene, Oregon, on a diet of jazz and soul, playing in a school band before discovering the blues. The Robert Cray Band was formed in 1974 and got its break when asked to back blues great Albert Collins on stage. The outfit cut its first album, *Who's Been Talking*, in 1980 and over succeeding releases built a steadily growing reputation. They even-tually won a place in the rock music first division, without in any way having to depart from the purity of approach to the blues—though there has always been an element of soul music in their work.

Apart from working with his band, Robert Cray has regularly jammed with Eric Clapton, Keith Richard, B. B. King, Chuck Berry and others and has evolved a fleet-fingered guitar style which is all his own.

The future of the blues is safe with superb singer/guitarists like Robert Cray.

PEE WEE CRAYTON

Like many of the best Texas bluesmen, Pee Wee Crayton found his fame and fortune out on America's West Coast, where he moved in his late teens. Truly a gifted guitarist, he bridged the gap between hard blues and commercial R&B, cutting a run of classy records and becoming a major star of Fifties and Sixties package shows on which he shared the bill with such major names as Roy Milton, Dinah Washington and Ray Charles.

Born in Rockdale, Texas, on December 18, 1914, Connie Curtis "Pee Wee" Crayton grew up in nearby Austin. He moved to California in 1935 and gradually felt his way into the local music scene, forming his own trio in 1945 and backing Ivory Joe Hunter on both gigs and recording dates. He recorded in his own right for 4-Star in 1947 and for Modern in 1949 before his classic period with Aladdin and Imperial.

Having gone into semi-retirement in the late Sixties, only working weekend dates, Pee Wee joined the Johnny Otis Show for the 1970 Monterey Jazz Festival and toured with Johnny for some time, as well as recording with Joe Turner, before his death on June 25, 1985.

ARTHUR "BIG BOY" CRUDUP

With his brand of raw country blues having faded from popularity, Arthur Crudup's never easy career seemed on the skids in 1954 but then something remarkable happened—an aspiring young white artist named Elvis Presley chose to cover his 'That's Alright' as one of his first sides for Sun. That record not only launched "the King"—it earned well-deserved credit and songwriting royalties for one of the greatest of the Mississippi Delta bluesmen, though it was to be many years before Arthur actually saw any of the money.

Earning the epithet "Big Boy" for his huge stature, Arthur Crudup grew up in Forest, Mississippi, where he had been born on August 25, 1905, the illegitimate son of musical parents. Though he lived up north in Indianapolis between the ages of 11 and 21, Arthur's Mississippi roots were deep and he returned to Forest in 1926 to work at local parties and juke joints.

Personal problems led him to flee to Chicago in 1940. He spent several years roughing it, living under the 39th Street "L" station and singing on street corners, until spotted at a party by talent scout Lester Melrose, who took him to RCA Records' Bluebird label. The eerie 'Death Valley Blues' earned Arthur a long-term contract which yielded such classics as 'Mean Ol' Frisco', 'Rock Me Mama', 'Look On Yonder's Wall' and 'That's Alright'.

Returning south, Arthur worked in the early Fifties with Elmore James, Sonny Boy Williamson and others. It was Arthur who, as Elmer James, cut the follow-up to Elmore's 'Dust My Broom' hit for Diamond.

The blues boom eventually brought him to the UK in 1970 and his fortunes revived but on March 28, 1974, he suffered a stroke and died at Nassawadox, Virginia.

REVD BLIND GARY DAVIS

Hard-drinking, cigar-smoking and living the life of a travelling minstrel, the Revd Blind Gary Davis was a most unusual minister but he worked the streets of New York's Harlem for more than 70 years until his death from a heart attack *en route* to a New Jersey date on May 5, 1972.

Born in Laurens County, South Carolina, on April 30, 1896, he suffered ulcerated eyes and lost most of his sight when just two months old, going totally blind by 1926. Gary taught himself harmonica at 5, banjo at 6 and guitar at 7. At 16, he developed a wanderlust, working the streets for nickels and dimes and coming into contact with those other great blind bluesmen, Blind Boy Fuller—with whom he made his first records—and Sonny Terry.

Gary became an ordained minster with the Missionary Baptist Connection Church after moving to New York City in 1940. He taught at Brownie McGhee's Home of the Blues Music School and worked steadily as an itinerant preacher, street musician and occasional recording artist until "discovered" by the Sixties blues boom.

Belated royalties from Elvis Presley covers of his songs brought Arthur Crudup long overdue reward for his creativity.

JIMMY "FAST FINGERS" DAWKINS

The consummate blues guitar stylist, Jimmy Dawkins has more than earned his epithet of "Fast Fingers". His work on sessions for Sonny Thompson, Johnny Young, "Wild Child" Butler, Koko Taylor, Carey Bell, Luther Allison and others eventually led to his own album début for Delmark in 1968. Since then, he has won a strong following for his plaintive, falsetto-heavy vocals and a guitar

Chicago's peerless blues tradition continues with fine musicians like Jimmy Dawkins.

style which, in the words of *Coda* magazine's Doug Langille, has "proved that the blues can evolve creatively yet be perpetuated in a relevant manner".

A native of Tchula, Mississippi, where he was born on October 24, 1936, Jimmy moved to Chicago in 1955, two years after he started guitar playing. He frequently worked club dates with Jimmy Rogers and Magic Sam.

In later years he worked with the Otis Rush band and visited Europe with the Chicago Blues Festival package.

WILLIE DIXON

One of the greatest songwriters in black America and a true catalyst of so much that was good on the Chicago blues scene, bass player Willie Dixon was far more important in terms of his contributions to other people's records than he was for his own rather spasmodic output. Muddy Waters, Howlin' Wolf, Jimmy Rogers, Sonny Boy Williamson, Bo Diddley, Chuck Berry, Koko Taylor and a host of others benefited from his formidable talents and Willie was a crucial element in the dramatic success of Chess Records as *the* blues label of the Fifties and Sixties.

His songs, including 'Little Red Rooster', 'Hoochie Coochie Man', 'My Babe', 'Spoonful' and 'Back Door Man', rate among the greatest of blues classics.

Willie James Dixon was born in Vicksburg, Mississippi, on July 1, 1915. After moving to Chicago, he won early fame as the Golden Gloves heavyweight boxing champ. Switching to music, he recorded for Bluebird in 1937 as a member of the Three Breezes, then worked as leader of the Four Jumps of Jive before forming the Big Three trio with Leonard Caston and Bernardo Dennis.

Willie landed a role as A&R man, talent scout, songwriter, arranger and producer with Aristocrat, which soon became Chess. Though making occasional forays outside the company—especially for his own recordings—he remained a cornerstone of Chess's success for many years and was possibly the single most influential personality in modern blues. He died in 1991.

CHAMPION JACK DUPREE

It was Jack Dupree's ability as a boxer—veteran of 107 professional bouts—that led to him being known as "Champion". It also said much for his redoubtable abilities as a keyboard maestro and highly individual vocalist. It was a style honed in the bawdy barrelhouses of New Orleans, the city where he was born on July 4, 1910, to a Cherokee Indian mother and a father of part French heritage. After his parents died in a fire, Jack was placed in the Coloured Waifs' Home for Boys.

Jack worked local dives as a singer/pianist through the Twenties then, after hoboing across America and his stint in boxing, made his first records for the OKeh label in Chicago in 1940, and served with the US Navy in the Pacific. After the war, Jack settled in New York, recording for a variety of companies including, notably, Folkways, Savoy, King, Groove and Atlantic.

In 1958 he toured Europe, where he became a big name, recording for Atlantic in London and for Sonet and Storyville in Copenhagen, eventually setting up home in Zurich in 1960. By 1965, Jack had moved to Copenhagen, continuing to work all over the Continent and in the UK, where he recorded with John Mayall.

Twice widowed, the veteran moved to Halifax, Yorkshire, in 1971 with his third wife, Shirley, an English girl. In 1971, he recorded in Paris with Mickey "Guitar" Baker and in 1974 moved base again, to Ballerup, Sweden. He died in 1991.

Bringing humour to the blues, Champion Jack Dupree was one of the music's true originals.

SNOOKS EAGLIN

Unusually for a New Orleans artist, Fird "Snooks" Eaglin opted for guitar rather than piano as his chosen instrument. Moreover, he worked mainly in an acoustic country style rather than the urban mode which might have been expected of a city boy.

Considerably younger than the first generation of country bluesmen—he was born in New Orleans on January 21, 1936—he counted a wide range of guitar styles and a warm and sensitive voice among his considerable assets. Blinded by glaucoma at 19 months of age, Snooks taught himself to play guitar when just 6 years old and frequently performed gospel songs in local churches before winning a talent competition on the local WNOE radio station in 1947.

He frequently worked with the Flamingoes R&B group and as a solo, beginning his recording career with Folkways in 1958, putting out a number of acclaimed albums, and visiting the UK in 1975.

SLEEPY JOHN ESTES

One of the greatest country blues artists, Sleepy John Estes sang and played with compelling intensity.

Born in Ripley, Tennessee, on January 25, 1899, he was blinded in his right eye by a baseball accident when he was 6. Growing up in an impoverished farming community, he learned to play on a homemade guitar constructed from a cigar box.

Teaming up with first Yank Rachell then Hammie Nixon, Sleepy John worked picnics and dances in the Brownsville area through the Twenties before being recorded by Victor in Memphis during 1929. Sleepy John frequently visited Chicago for recording sessions and club dates during the Thirties and Forties.

Completely blind by 1950, he spent some years based in Memphis, recording for Sun at the same time as people like B. B. King, Junior Parker and Howlin' Wolf were in that city laying the ground rules for the highly amplified urban blues style. Sleepy John, however, stayed true to his roots and stuck with the acoustic style right through to his death of a stroke on June 5, 1977, in Brownsville.

FLEETWOOD MAC

Though they have gone through numerous personnel changes and an evolution into the world's most successful pop/rock band, Fleetwood Mac started out back in 1967 as a purist blues band aping the Chicago tradition. Ace guitarist Peter Green formed the outfit with drummer Mick Fleetwood and bass player John McVie, who had just been fired by John Mayall, and a second guitarist, Jeremy Spencer.

Folk hero Jesse Fuller saved on musicians' fees by doing it all himself.

Unable to interest Decca in the band, producer Mike Vernon quit the company to set up his own Blue Horizon label which went on to release product by many major American blues artists. The *Blues Jam At Chess* album saw Fleetwood Mac recording in their spiritual home in Chicago—by which time they had added a third guitarist, Danny Kirwan. First Green, then Spencer left the band to join cult religious sects and from then on the outfit moved out of the blues mainstream.

JESSE "LONE CAT" FULLER

The one-man band tradition was strong in the early evolution of the blues, its exponents including Dr Isaiah Ross, Joe Hill Louis, Sam "Stovepipe no. 1" Jones and Jesse Fuller. Jesse Fuller's chosen instrumentation comprised 12-string

acoustic guitar, harmonica, kazoo, washboard and fotdella, an extremely strange stringed instrument played with the big toe of the right foot.

His childhood was bleak. He never knew his father and there is no record of his birth, though he believed it to have been in Jonesboro, near Atlanta, Georgia, on March 12, 1896. Raised by the Wilson family, who sadistically mistreated him, Jesse ran away as a 10-year-old and worked at various jobs, besides playing street music. He arrived in California in 1922, working on Hollywood movie lots as a labourer and eventually settling in the Bay Area at the end of the decade. Jesse worked local clubs, sometimes with Leadbelly, but did not make it on to record until after the Second World War had ended.

Suddenly discovered by folk music fans, he was elevated to international cult status in the late Fifties, an audience of

4,500 attending a concert in Islington, London, while fans in Belfast hoisted him on to their shoulders in triumph. Further European visits and US folk festival appearances kept him busy throughout the Sixties but by 1971 ill-health was curtailing his musical activities and he died of heart disease in an Oakland, California, hospital on January 29, 1976, age 80.

LOWELL FULSOM

Though his name has usually been put on record labels as Fulsom, the sometimes used alternative spelling of Fulson was actually the correct surname of an artist over whose class there is no doubt.

Born on an Indian reservation near Tulsa, Oklahoma, on March 31, 1921, the son of a black woman and a full-blood Cherokee, Lowell learned guitar at 12. He left home in the late Thirties to work with Dan Wright's String Band and occasionally play country and western music. Meeting up with Texas Alexander in 1939, he became that artist's guitar player for a year.

On returning from naval service and settling in Oakland, California, he was signed by Big Town Records' boss Bob Geddins after having been drawn into the latter's radio repair shop by the sounds of guitar playing coming from inside.

During a 3-year stint with Geddins, Lowell cut urban blues and also recorded country blues material with support from his brother Martin on acoustic guitar.

Lowell's rather sophisticated approach, with relaxed rhythms and gently rolling guitar, appealed to the burgeoning Swing Time label in LA. By 1952, they had made him an established star, with such classics as 'Everyday I Have The Blues' and 'Blue Shadows' to his credit, using the talented Lloyd Glenn as his pianist and carrying a ten-piece road band which included Ray Charles and Stanley Turrentine among its luminaries. In 1954, Lowell topped the R&B charts with the haunting 'Reconsider Baby', on Checker, while subsequent records for Kent included the superb 'Black Nights' and 'Tramp', the latter covered by Stax soul stars Otis Redding and Carla Thomas.

In 1968, Jewel Records' boss, Stan Lewis, sent Lowell to the Fame Studios in Muscle Shoals, Alabama, to record with the hottest studio band in soul music.

The idea reflected the crossover nature of Lowell's brand of R&B, which has continued to this day, 1991 finding him recording for the first time with Jimmy McCracklin, a friend of 20 years who has also worked this rich vein.

BUDDY GUY

Growing up in Lettsworth, Louisiana, where he was born on July 30, 1936, George "Buddy" Guy learned to play on a homemade guitar at 13 and by 1953 was gigging

A favourite of the Rolling Stones, fleet-fingered Buddy Guy is a giant of the Chicago style of amplified blues.

regularly with Lightnin' Slim, Lazy Lester, Slim Harpo and other local stars.

By 1957 he had moved to Chicago, enjoying early encouragement from Muddy Waters and sitting in with Otis Rush before forming his own trio.

Within a year, Buddy had won a "Battle of the Blues" competition at the Blue Flame Club, beating Otis Rush, Junior Wells and Magic Sam, with which latter artist he recorded for Cobra before recording his own band for Artistic. Willie Dixon took him to Chess in 1960 and he became regular house guitarist for the label, as well as making his own records.

Striking up a loose partnership with harmonica player Junior Wells, which has lasted on-and-off to present times, he recorded for Vanguard through the Sixties, often using his brother Phil as a sideman. In 1970, Buddy toured with the Rolling Stones, reflecting his reputation as one of the most polished showmen of the blues—an inspired guitarist and powerful singer.

JOHN HAMMOND JR.

Though he is son of the Columbia Records' talent scout John Hammond who produced the near-legendary *Spirituals To Swing* concerts at Carnegie Hall in the late Thirties, John Hammond Jr. (who has also worked as John Paul Hammond) discovered the blues for himself, his parents having separated when he was young. Soon becoming an avid record collector, he taught himself guitar and harmonica while studying at the Antoich College in Yellow Springs, Ohio.

After playing in Los Angeles coffee houses, John returned to New York where he quickly established himself on the fast-burgeoning folk blues scene of the mid-Sixties as one of its most authentic exponents, despite his white middle-class upbringing. A master of all the subtleties and stylistic idiosyncrasies of the classic Mississippi Delta blues tradition, he in 1992 presented the remarkable *Search For Robert Johnson* TV documentary.

SLIM HARPO

With his lazy, laid-back, half-mumbled delivery, hypnotic guitar sound and insistently repetitive harmonica, Slim Harpo almost single-handedly defined the distinctive Louisiana swamp blues style which also brought success to the likes of Lazy Lester, Silas Hogan and Arthur Gunter. Sadly, Slim died of a heart attack, in Baton Rouge, Louisiana, on January 31, 1970, at the early age of 46, just when interest in his work was reaching a new height.

Born in West Baton Rouge on January 11, 1924, he dropped out of school to work as a musician after his parents died and by the early Forties was well known throughout his home state playing in the clubs under the alias of Harmonica Slim.

Signed to Excello Records by Jay Miller after having first worked in the company's Crowley, Louisiana, studio accompanying Lightnin' Slim (Otis Hicks), who had married his sister, Slim Harpo brought the company immediate success.

For his first release, the insistent 'I Got Love If You Want It' was coupled with 'King Bee', a song which became his theme, as well as entering the repertoire of countless American and British blues acts.

In 1961, the more relaxed 'Raining In My Heart' topped the American R&B charts and his superb follow-ups and consequent fame earned Slim a slot on a major James Brown concert date at the prestigious Madison Square Gardens in 1966. After that, things quietened down and he went back to working local club dates and running his own trucking business.

A début visit to Europe for the summer of 1970 was being arranged when news broke of his premature death.

PEPPERMINT HARRIS

Though he worked prolifically through the Fifties and up until the mid-Sixties, leaving a rich storehouse of fine records, little is known of Peppermint Harris's background. He is believed to have been born somewhere in Texas sometime around 1925, his real name being Harrison Nelson.

After recording for Gold Star, Sittin' In With, Modern and Time in Houston between 1947 and 1951, Peppermint moved to the West Coast to cut hits in Los Angeles for Aladdin, Money and X. In 1955 he was cutting sides for Dart Records in Lake Charles, Louisiana,

and by 1962 he was back in Texas, recording in Houston for Don Robey's Duke label. In 1955–6, he had releases on Jewel but then, reportedly, took up work outside the music industry, moving from Houston to Chicago to New Orleans to Texarkana, Arkansas, in 1970, from which point he dropped out of sight.

A classy performer, Peppermint Harris—along with Pee Wee Crayton, Clarence "Gatemouth" Brown and Albert Collins—represented the generation of Texas blues artists which followed on from Lightnin' Hopkins and Smokey Hogg and preceded current exponents like Johnny Watson and Johnny Copeland.

WYNONIE HARRIS

One of the great blues shouters, Wynonie Harris owned a set of vocal cords which one admiring critic likened to being made of steel.

University educated, Wynonie was born in Omaha, Nebraska, and was just about the only blues artist of any note to have come from that part of the USA. He started his show-business career as a comedian and dancer before teaching himself drums and forming a combo.

Moving to Los Angeles to work as an MC and singer at the Club Alabam, he appeared as a dancer in the movie *Hit Parade of 1943* and frequently produced stage shows. After working with the Lucky Millinder Orchestra at the Savoy Ballroom, Wynonie went to New York City to record with them for Decca.

Fronting big bands led by Illinois Jacquet, Jack McVea, Oscar Pettiford, Lionel Hampton, Johnny Otis and others, he toured and recorded prolifically—notably for Aladdin and King—before moving to the East Coast in 1953, retiring from music and running his own café in Brooklyn, New York.

Wynonie returned to recording in 1963, at which time he also shifted his base west back to LA, where he owned another café. His last big appearance was at Harlem's Apollo Theatre in 1967 and he died of cancer back in Los Angeles on June 14, 1969.

SMOKEY HOGG

It was the combined effect of cancer and an over-fondness for alcohol which killed Andrew "Smokey" Hogg on May 1, 1960. He was just 46 when his family buried him at the cemetery in Westconnie, the small Texas community where he had been born on January 27, 1914.

Encouraged by his first cousin, Lightnin' Hopkins, and nicknamed "Little Peetie Wheatstraw" because he sounded so much like the star, Smokey worked throughout Texas until a talent scout arrived to take him up to Chicago to record for Decca in 1937. Following another cousin, John Hogg, to Los Angeles, in 1947, he worked with Frankie Lee Sims and recorded for Exclusive, Bullet, Modern, Specialty and Imperial over the following years. Sadly, his death happened before the blues revival which would surely have made him a big name in Europe.

Remembered as a slow, simple man who always had a bottle by his side, Smokey had great difficulty keeping time with his accompanists, but the innate charm of his straightforward but distinctive style always shone through.

BILLIE HOLIDAY

Though dubbed "the Voice of Jazz", Billie Holiday had a style which boasted strong blues leanings—the rather distorted film of her life story, starring Diana Ross, being titled *The Lady Sings the Blues*.

Born in Baltimore, Maryland, in 1915, Billie, whose recordings through the Thirties featured the cream of jazz musicians, including Lester Young, Ben Webster and Roy Eldridge and the big bands of Duke Ellington, Count Basie and Fletcher Henderson, was a major influence over most women blues singers. Her macabre 'Strange Fruit', recorded in 1939, is on its own sufficient to justify her inclusion in any blues hall of fame.

A troubled woman, having suffered racial prejudice, broken marriage and other personal problems, including narcotics convictions, Billie died in July 1959 at Metropolitan Hospital, New York, of drug poisoning.

Underrated but one of the very best—the late Earl Hooker.

EARL HOOKER

A cousin of both John Lee Hooker and soul artist Joe Hinton, and a nephew of Kansas City Red, Earl Zebedee Hooker was born at Clarksdale, Mississippi, on January 15, 1930. He moved to Chicago in 1941 to attend music school.

Robert Nighthawk taught him guitar technique and took him to Helena, Arkansas for appearances on Sonny Boy Williamson's *King Biscuit Time* radio show.

In the early Fifties, Earl toured as a member of Ike Turner's Kings of Rhythm and recorded in Memphis for Rockin' and King before setting up his own band. Though his schedule was often interrupted by ill health, Earl became a major figure on the Chicago scene, working with the likes of Otis Rush, Junior Parker, Junior Wells and his own band as well as appearing on the same *Ready Steady Go* TV show bill in London as the Beatles.

On April 21, 1970, Earl died in Chicago of pulmonary tuberculosis. He had been one of the finest, if sadly under-appreciated, of modern bluesmen.

JOHN LEE HOOKER

See separate entry in the Legends section.

SAM "LIGHTNIN'" HOPKINS

In his youth, Lightnin' Hopkins was greatly influenced by his brother Joel, his cousin Texas Alexander and, even more importantly, by the legendary Blind Lemon Jefferson, with all of whom he played. While spending most of his life based in big city Houston, he remained true to the country blues idiom, developing his own quirky singing and guitar style, with added tap-dance style rhythm coming from shoe soles studded with beer-bottle tops.

He had been born at Centreville, Texas, on March 15, 1912, and spent time at a prison farm in the Thirties. In 1946, his woman manager, Lola Ann Cullum, took him out to California. Lightnin' became an immediate star, recording hundreds of sides for a wide range of labels until 1954 when, overnight, rock 'n' roll rendered his kind of music obsolete among black audiences.

It was folklorist Mack McCormick who revived Lightnin's career in 1959. He again recorded prolifically, his music being promoted to the burgeoning market among white blues addicts worldwide. He remained popular until his death on January 3, 1982.

McCormick summed up Lightnin's appeal: "He is—in the finest sense of the word—a minstrel: a street-singing, improvising songmaker born to the vast tradition of the blues. His music is as personal as a hushed conversation."

BIG WALTER "SHAKEY" HORTON

Rated firmly in the front rank of Chicago harmonica players for many years, Big Walter "Shakey" Horton added his powerhouse playing to records by many of the greats—including Muddy Waters and Big Mama Thornton—as well as recording prolifically on his own account.

Self-taught at just 5 years of age, by his teens Walter was already entertaining the crowds at dances and country picnics around Horn Lake, Mississippi, where he had been born on April 6, 1917. After moving to Memphis, he worked steadily with the Memphis Jug Band through the late Twenties and moved with them to Chicago in 1927, recording with the act for Victor when he was just 10 years old.

Returning to Memphis and teaming up with Homesick James and others, Walter worked the streets and clubs there and in Chicago during the Thirties and Forties. Having already recorded for Modern, Sun and Chess, in 1953 Walter started a long-term casual working relationship with Johnny Shines.

By 1965, Walter had widened his audience to Europe, taking part in the American Folk Blues Festival that year and returning with the package in 1968 and 1970. He remained a giant of the Chicago blues hierarchy through the Seventies and died in 1981.

EDDIE "SON" HOUSE

Though in many ways the father of the Delta style of blues—as mentor of Robert Johnson, Muddy Waters and others—Son House was unable to earn a full-time living from music until the folk blues revival brought him out of a 10-year retirement in 1964, taking him as far away as Europe to play.

Son's intense, anguished style was born in the cottonfields of Mississippi, where he grew up on a

With his brooding bottleneck style, Son House inspired the greats, despite being only a part-time musician.

plantation between Clarksdale and Lyon, having been born in Riverton on March 21, 1902. After a short spell in East St Louis, he returned to Mississippi in 1923 and played at parties and picnics with Charlie Patton and others, served time at Parchman State Farm prison and, in

1930, made his first recordings, for Paramount Records. In 1941 and 1942, Alan Lomax recorded Son for the Library of Congress with Son's long-time friend Willie Brown as accompanist.

Moving to Rochester, New York, in 1943, Son was inactive in music until the Washington-based Blue Goose label sought him out a decade later and he started working the folk circuits. He died on October 19, 1988.

MISSISSIPPI JOHN HURT

A colourful character, Mississippi John Hurt played appropriately rich-hued music, his brilliant guitar-picking and hypnotic vocals enhanced by a consummate sense of phrasing and emotional communication.

From his birth at Teoc, Mississippi, on July 3, 1893, until the Sixties, he lived and worked in obscurity until, suddenly discovered by the folk blues revivalists, he became a much loved star—at more than 70 years of age.

Though the good times took him as far as Johnny Carson's prime-time networked *Tonight* TV show, and acclaim at the famed Newport Folk Festival, they were not to last long. He died of a heart attack, on November 2, 1966, at his home in Grenada, Mississippi.

Behind him, Mississippi John left a legacy of obscure 78s—the first released by OKeh in 1928—and some fine latter-day albums, mostly on Vanguard, all of which most ably captured the essential spirit of the Mississippi Delta blues heartland.

Country blues giant Mississippi John Hurt lived a life as rich as his remarkable music.

ELMORE JAMES

See separate entry in the Legends section.

ETTA JAMES

Etta James's prolific output has included rock 'n' roll, R&B, gospel, soul and disco, yet it has all been hallmarked by that remarkable raw-edged blues voice.

Born in Los Angeles in 1938, she was a 15-year old, singing in the Peaches trio with two sisters when they were discovered by blues Svengali Johnny Otis who granted them an after-the-show audition at a San Francisco hotel. Produced by Otis for Modern Records, the novelty song 'Roll With Me Henry' gave Etta an instant R&B smash and made her a teen star.

Quitting the Otis Revue, Etta made her way to Chicago, at the urging of Harvey Fuqua, of Harvey and the Moonglows, and came under the wing of Leonard Chess, who signed her to his Argo label. The heart-rending 'All I Could Do Was Cry' was followed by a string of 18 hits, including duets with Sugar Pie DeSanto.

With sales flagging, Chess sent Etta to Muscle Shoals in 1967, where she recorded the original and definitive version of the 'I'd Rather Go Blind' classic. Etta's career was reborn in the Nineties with a string of fine albums which took her closer to the blues mainstream but, at the same time, appealed to rock audiences worldwide.

HOMESICK JAMES

Born John A. Williamson on April 30, 1910 at Somerville, Tennessee, Homesick James was the illegitimate son of a musician named Henderson. He taught himself to play on his mother's guitar, running away at 12 to hobo around Tennessee. By 14, he had got to North Carolina, where he met and learned from the original Blind Boy Fuller, who was two years older and more accomplished. He also worked with Sleepy John Estes, Frank Stokes and others, moving to Chicago in 1926, when his parents came searching for him.

Seeking out Big Bill Broonzy and Lonnie Johnson and learning from them, he gigged extensively in St Louis and Memphis—where he made his first record, for Victor, in 1934—as well as in his adopted hometown of Chicago. In 1951, he recorded 'Homesick', which led to his nickname.

From 1954 he worked with his cousin Elmore James's band and played on many of Elmore's biggest hits, including 'Dust My Blues' and 'The Sky Is Crying'. When Elmore died of a heart attack in 1964, Homesick James went back to running his own band, playing in a similar bottleneck style and making 'Crossroads' his own—and much imitated—theme.

SKIP JAMES

The son of a preacher, Nehemiah "Skip" James not surprisingly displayed a very strong gospel influence in his music, making him one of the most distinctive of all the great acoustic country bluesmen.

Though born in the heart of the Delta country on a plantation near Bentonia, Mississippi, on June 9, 1920, he only knew his peers like Charlie Patton, Son House, Bukka White and Robert Johnson through their records. He worked at different periods with Henry Stuckey and Johnnie Temple in joints during the Twenties and Thirties while also, on moving to Dallas, forming the Dallas Texas Jubilee Singers. He became an ordained minister in 1946 and moved back to rural Mississippi.

Rediscovered during the great blues revival, he worked folk clubs and blues concerts and visited Europe during the Sixties, before succumbing to cancer and dying on October 3, 1969 at Philadelphia, Pennsylvania.

BLIND LEMON JEFFERSON

The marker placed by blues enthusiasts on Blind Lemon Jefferson's grave at the Negro Cemetery in Wortham, Texas, acclaims him as "one of America's outstanding original musicians"—a judgement which few would dispute. Though he spent most of his life in poverty, Blind Lemon was one of the biggest-selling of all black recording artists during the period 1925–30. A true folk poet, with a haunting voice, he helped define the acoustic country blues form and penned many of its most memorable songs.

Blind Lemon was born during July, 1897, at Couchman, Texas, the son of a farmer. Sightless from birth, he earned his keep as a beggar and itinerant musician, working the streets of Dallas, Galveston, Houston and other Texas towns from 1912 onwards and being taken north to Chicago to work rent parties once his records began to spread his fame.

His first 78s were gospel items for Paramount but it was his blues records, for that label and OKeh, which spread his fame—though they failed to make his fortune.

Sometime in December 1929, Blind Lemon collapsed of a heart attack on a Chicago sidewalk and reportedly died of exposure. His body was returned to his hometown and buried in a pauper's grave which sadly went unmarked until 1967.

ROBERT JOHNSON

See separate entry in the Legends section.

JANIS JOPLIN

Making up in sheer enthusiasm for what she might have lacked in finesse, Janis Joplin was a white fan of Bessie Smith and Leadbelly records who herself became one of the great blues belters during a short but eventful career which ended with her death from a drug overdose in Los Angeles on October 4, 1970.

Leaving Port Arthur, Texas, where she had been born on January 19, 1943 and worked with a bluegrass band singing a mix of country and blues, Janis settled in San Francisco's Haight Ashbury hippy district and became lead singer with Big Brother and the Holding Company. Her classic reading of Irma Thomas's soul gem 'Piece Of My Heart' revealed the depths of her emotions. While she too often resorted to histrionic screaming, Janis was undoubtedly a blues shouter of real ability. Her short life was the inspiration for the Bette Midler movie *The Rose*.

ALBERT KING

Though early publicity linked them—B. B. King's father's name also happens to be Albert, and the two blues giants were both born in the same Mississippi Delta district of Indianola, Mississippi—there was no blood relationship between B.B. and Albert King.

There is, however, a common heritage and both men have been enormously influential on fellow bluesmen and white rock artists alike. When Albert's death of a heart attack was announced from a Memphis hospital on December 21, 1992, Wayne Jackson of the Memphis

Bringing the blues flavour to the West Coast rock scene, Janis Joplin oozed emotion.

Horns proclaimed him as "one of the most important guitar players who ever lived".

One of 13 children, his real name was Albert Nelson. He was two years older than B. B. King, having been born on April 25, 1923. Moving to the Forest City–Osceola area to work as a plantation labourer as well as singing with the Harmony Kings gospel group, Albert had lived away from home for almost a decade before he taught himself to play guitar and, from 1939, began working the roadhouses as a blues artist. On moving to Gary, Indiana, he worked as a drummer with Jimmy Reed, Earl Hooker and other Chicago stalwarts before moving to St Louis, starting his own combo and recording for Bobbin, King and Count-Tree, with Ike Turner often his producer.

The big break came in 1965 when he was signed to Stax Records who put him in the studios with Booker T And The MGs for a brilliant album which headlined 'Born Under A Bad Sign', a number co-written by Booker T. Jones. The magic *Memphis Sound* worked wonders for Albert, who quickly became a blues superstar with his hallmark rocket-shaped guitar, strung upside down and played left-handed.

Later recordings for Tomato, including the brilliant *Truck Load Of Lovin'* album, ranked among the finest samples of modern blues/R&B at its most intense. Eric Clapton, Jimi Hendrix, Jimmy Page and Taj Mahal were among the many greats who played tribute to the 6-foot 4-inch, 250-lb giant's influence.

...XIS KORNER
...CYRIL DAVIES

...x, half-Austrian descent, Alexis
...laying country blues with Cyril
...ack as 1955—calling it skiffle. They
...ed their style until, in the early
...lues Incorporated became the sem-
...he entire British R&B movement,
...vay for the Rolling Stones, the
... John Baldry, John Mayall, Them and

...he Mississippi-rooted hard-rocking Chicago
..., during the heyday of its residency at Ealing
...vas as hot as the real thing, with Korner's
...vies's stunning harmonica work and vocals
... the superb saxophone of Dick Heckstall-
...her Charlie Watts (later of the Stones) or
... (later of Cream) on drums. A fluid cast
...l Jones (later of Manfred Mann fame), Long
...nd others also sharing the stand.
...orporated's *Rhythm & Blues From The*
...n remains, arguably, the finest album
...l by a non-American blues band while
...Cyril Davies All-Stars' instrumental

...raconteur and musician—Alexis Korner was a
...itish blues and R&B movement.

B.

See separate

FRE

Guitar-wizard-to-be
moved to Chicago fr
been born on Septen
ting in with other art
Blues Boys with Jimm
ing dates for Parrot
Cooper in 1953. By
leading talent scout S

Between 1961 and
studios in Cincinnati yi
the biggest was the dr
career went into the
most notably Eric Cla
Subsequent recordings
and Shelter, a label ru
made him a powerhou

Freddie toured wo
cumbed to hepatitis ar
the early age of 42.

Born under a bad sign, maybe, b
Albert King.

AL

AND

Of half-Gree
Korner was
Davies as far l
gradually hor
Sixties, their
inal band of
paving the
Animals, Lor
many more.

Working
style, the ban
Blues Club,
guitar and D
supported by
Smith and ei
Ginger Bake
also found Pa
John Baldry

Blues In
Marquee albu
ever record
the frenetic

Broadcaster, write
key figure in the

single 'Country Line Special' is not only a classic but a highly original record which added something to the Chicago blues idiom, rather than being merely derivative.

Cyril Davies, who was born in 1932, died of leukemia on January 7, 1964. Alexis Korner, who had been born in Paris on April 19, 1928, died on January 1, 1984, after having served many years as a DJ, writer and general guru of the British blues movement.

HUDDIE "LEADBELLY" LEDBETTER

A notorious womanizer and convicted killer, the hulking enigma that was Huddie Ledbetter claimed his sobriquet of "Leadbelly" was earned as a result of gunshot wounds—though it was more likely merely a corruption of his surname. Like Big Bill Broonzy—who boasted of being "the last surviving country blues singer" when countless other superb artists were still in the Deep South awaiting discovery—Leadbelly was a great weaver of myths and fantasies, claiming, among other things, that he twice sang his way out of prison! One thing that cannot be denied is that he made a tremendous contribution to keeping interest in country blues alive—even if he died a decade before the revival movement got underway.

Various dates for his birth at Mooringsport, Louisiana, have been given, of which January 20, 1889, seems the most reliable.

Leadbelly was one of several major artists to be who came under the influence of Blind Lemon Jefferson in Dallas during the Twenties. Besides playing 12-string guitar, he was already proficient on accordion, bass, harmonica and piano.

His first recordings, supervised by Alan and John Lomax for the Library of Congress, were made during 1933 and 1934 at Angola State Prison, in Louisiana, where he was serving a sentence for attempted murder, having already been imprisoned in 1917 for killing a man at New Boston, Texas, and returning to jail in 1939 for assault.

After a spell as John Lomax's driver, travelling through the eastern and southern states, Leadbelly moved to New York and managed to break into the folk circuit, working with fellow blues artists Josh White, Sonny Terry and Brownie McGhee and white artist Woody Guthrie. By 1945 he was hosting his own West Coast radio show. He also performed in Paris shortly before his death in New York on December 6, 1949.

Leadbelly in typically moody pose, ever aware of his tough image.

J. B. LENOIR

Some time in the mid-Sixties, an odd and amazingly simple little blues ditty called 'I Sing Um The Way I Feel' set the London discotheque dancefloors alight. It was the first those mod crowds had ever heard of J. B. Lenoir, and their enthusiasm for his novel sound won him a showcase place on the 1965 American Folk Blues Festival tour of the UK and Europe.

Hardcore followers of the Chicago blues scene already knew him as something more than a mere one-hit-wonder. J.B.—who was born at Montecello, Mississippi, on March 5, 1929 (the initials J.B. do not stand for anything and were his given name)—had been active since the late Thirties when he worked at various southern venues with Elmore James and Sonny Boy Williamson.

Migrating to Chicago in 1949, J.B. was a regular on the club scene, frequently appearing alongside Memphis Minnie, Big Maceo, Muddy Waters and Big Bill Broonzy. He formed J.B. And His Bayou Boys and began recording for Chess in 1949, with following sides appearing on JOB, Parrot and other labels.

Following his American Folk Blues Festival success of 1965, J.B. was back in Europe the next year but, on April 29, 1967 at Urbana, Illinois, he died from a heart attack brought on by a car crash.

MANCE LIPSCOMB

Although he had been a musician from childhood, Mance Lipscomb had never played professionally before being discovered for Arhoolie Records by blues researcher Mack McCormick, in 1960.

The son of a one-time slave, Mance was born on a farm near Navasota, Texas, on April 9, 1895. Though his new-found fame was to take him all over America during the great blues revival boom years, Mance's heart and home remained in the South, where he had learned his trade playing at suppers, barn dances and school hops.

His intensely rural style contained elements of the field hollers, reels, breakdowns and worksongs which predated the blues and the singer/guitarist summed himself up succinctly as "a songster".

Though he had never recorded until he was 65, he came to be regarded as one of the finest exponents of the rural blues sound. Mance died of coronary illness on January 30, 1976 at his home town of Navasota.

PROFESSOR LONGHAIR

Affectionately known to connoisseurs of the New Orleans scene as simply "Fess", Roy "Professor Longhair" Byrd was described by Robert Palmer as "the most colourful and influential pianist to emerge from the New Orleans milieu since Jelly Roll Morton".

Piano-pounding Professor Longhair influenced several generations of New Orleans musicians.

A father-figure to James Booker, Mac "Dr. John" Rebennack, Huey "Piano" Smith, Allen Toussaint and other Crescent City piano-pumping talents, he was born in Bogalusa, Louisiana, on December 18, 1918 and raised in New Orleans where he worked as both a pianist and a guitarist from the late Twenties.

A real character, Fess supplemented his musical income with employment in the Civilian Conservation Corps and his earnings from professional gambling. He began recording in 1949.

Though a major figure for years in his hometown, it was not until the Seventies that Professor Longhair became more widely known, thanks to the praise heaped on him by Dr. John and others. He made numerous European visits—recording in London for Harvest in 1977—up until his death in New Orleans on January 30, 1980.

CHARLIE McCOY

A prolific accompanist on both guitar and mandolin, as well as a recording artist in his own right, Charlie "Papa" McCoy did much to help define the direction popular blues music would take.

Born on May 26, 1909 in Jackson, Mississippi, he worked with Rubin Lacy, Walter Vinson, Tommy Johnson and others on the local club scene before visiting Chicago in the late Twenties to play house parties.

Charlie first recorded as a backing musician with Ishmon Bracey for the Victor label in 1928. Subsequent bookings found him recording in New Orleans with Bo Chatmon, in Atlanta with the Mississippi Black Snakes, and in his own right for Vocalion in New York and for Decca in Chicago in 1934–5. Much in demand, Charlie went on to accompany Bill Broonzy, Memphis Minnie, Frankie Jaxon, John Lee "Sonny Boy" Williamson and others, but mental health problems made him inactive from 1946 onwards. He entered psychiatric hospital and died on July 26, 1950 of paralytic brain disease.

JIMMY McCRACKLIN

A one-time All-American light heavyweight boxing champion and world title contender, with 21 consecutive knockouts to his credit, Jimmy McCracklin turned to music when a car accident ended his fighting career.

Singing had been his first love, starting out in church choirs in St Louis, Missouri, where he was born on August 13, 1931. Moving to the Watts district of Los Angeles in his teens, Jimmy made early recordings for local independents through the Forties before beginning his serious musical career after three years in the US Navy and his abortive bid for the top in boxing.

His first success came with 'The Walk' for Chess in 1957 and, on joining Imperial in 1961, the hits took off in earnest with the classic 'Just Got To Know'.

By the Seventies, when his Willie Mitchell-produced 'Yesterday Is Gone' album was issued by Stax, Jimmy had moved from the R&B/soul crossover style which had made him a star towards a more straightforward urban blues mode which has continued to the present time.

One-time world boxing championship contender Jimmy McCracklin has long been a heavyweight of the R&B scene.

MISSISSIPPI FRED McDOWELL

One of the great discoveries of the first folk blues revival of the late Fifties, Fred McDowell was to become the darling of the scene. Born at Rossville, Tennessee, on January 12, 1904, the son of a farmer, Fred worked as a farmhand and itinerant labourer, scuffling throughout the Mississippi Delta until his new life as a folk blues hero got under way.

Discovered initially by Alan Lomax, who was on a field trip for the Library of Congress in 1959, Fred cut sessions at Como, Mississippi, which were eventually released by Atlantic, on the epic *Sounds Of The South* compilation, and by Prestige. Five years later, other record companies took up the trail.

It had taken the affable Mississippi artist more than 30 years to become a success and get his music on to disc and across to an international audience, leading blues authority Pete Welding to comment: "Fred McDowell is a blues singer/guitarist of such extraordinary power, emotional intensity and strong individuality that he must be counted among the most significant discoveries of recent years."

From the mid-Sixties on, releases via Arhoolie, Testament, Vanguard, Polydor and a number of other labels, as well as steady concert and club work, kept him busy. Fred died of cancer in Memphis on July 3, 1972.

BLIND WILLIE McTELL

Almost totally blind from birth, William Samuel "Blind Willie" McTell moved from Thomson, Georgia, where he had been born on May 5, 1901, to Statesboro, Georgia, when he was 9, learning guitar from his musician mother. Like many youngsters of his era, he ran away from home at 13 to join a travelling minstrel show before attending schools for the blind, first in Macon, Georgia, then in New York City.

Working throughout the East Coast states, but usually ending up back in his native Georgia, Willie was an itinerant musician throughout the Thirties but managed to get on record, for Columbia, as early as 1929. Playing at parties, restaurants, clubs, dances, private parties and similar engagements, Willie managed to find plenty of work with his compelling imagery, deeply personal style and deft-fingered 12-string guitar plucking.

In 1959, he was admitted to Milledgeville State Hospital, in Georgia, where he died of a brain haemorrhage on August 19. Willie used various pseudonyms during his career, including Georgia Bill, Hot Shot Willie, Barrelhouse Sammy, Blind Doogie, Red Hot Willie, Pig 'n' Whistle Red, and Blind Sammy.

TAJ MAHAL

Born in New York City on May 17, 1940 (the son of a West Indian jazz musician father and a South Carolina-born gospel singer mother) and holder of a BA university degree, Taj Mahal once said: "Some people think you have to be Blind Lester Crawdad and come up the river from New Orleans and into Chicago to play good blues. But it's not indigenous to a time or place, the music is indigenous to the people."

Mixing roots with intellect—Taj Mahal has spread the blues message to a wide audience.

Since bursting on to the scene in 1967, with the best-selling eponymously titled Columbia album, Taj Mahal has explored every dimension of the blues tradition and taken it down new roads too, adding elements from Caribbean, South American and African folk music, and from jazz, soul and funk as well.

That first album was notable for the brilliant mandolin playing of Ry Cooder and Jesse Edwin Davis's lead guitar, with Taj playing slide guitar and harmonica.

On subsequent sessions, Taj has consistently used the best of musicians, white and black alike.

JOHN MAYALL

Not the greatest of singers or guitarists, John Mayall's part in the history of the blues lay more in his function as a catalyst, gathering around him some of the very finest players—British and American alike—and nurturing their talents.

Early experience for the British bandleader, who was born in Manchester on November 23, 1933, came with his Powerhouse Four combo, backing artists like John Lee Hooker and Sonny Boy Williamson on UK tours. In 1962, Alexis Korner encouraged Mayall to move to London, where he soon became part of the burgeoning R&B club scene at such venues as the Flamingo and Klooks Kleek at which latter club he cut his first album, live, in 1964.

John Mayall's Bluesbreakers became a major act when guitar wizard Eric Clapton left the Yardbirds to join the line-up. When Clapton moved on to form Cream, he was replaced by Peter Green while Mick Fleetwood joined on drums. Green and Fleetwood quit in 1967 along with original Bluesbreakers' bass player John McVie to start Fleetwood Mac.

After Mick Taylor left to join the Rolling Stones in 1968, John switched his base to Los Angeles, bringing many classy black American musicians—including, notably, Mel Brown—into his ever-evolving line-up.

BIG MAYBELLE

Respected UK blues and soul writer Dave Godin wrote of Big Maybelle: "When she sang, she was possessed by a magic that could drive out her own personal devils."

One of the great blues belters, Maybelle was big in name, size, personality and voice.

She was an institution at Harlem's famed Apollo Theatre and other venues for two decades, from the Fifties to her death in Cleveland, Ohio, on January 23, 1972 of a diabetic coma.

Born Mabel Louise Smith at Jackson, Tennessee, on May 1, 1924 and able to sing in four languages, Big Maybelle won a major Memphis talent contest in 1932 before touring with the Sweethearts Of Rhythm all-girl group, working throughout the state for the rest of the decade and into the Forties.

After recording with the Christine Chatman Orchestra for Decca in New York, Big Maybelle toured and recorded regularly with Tiny Bradshaw's big band from 1947 to 1950 before signing with King Records.

Subsequent releases on Savoy and OKeh and her set at the 1958 Newport Jazz Festival, part of which featured in the acclaimed *Jazz On A Summer's Day* movie, made Big Maybelle a major figure of the R&B scene. Sadly, ill-health drastically reduced her activities from 1967 through to her death five years later.

PERCY MAYFIELD

Almost as well known for the hits he wrote for others— including 'Hit The Road Jack' and other memorable songs for Ray Charles who, at one time, retained him

Big Maybelle had a powerful voice and on-stage persona to match her physical stature.

as a staff writer for his Tangerine label—Percy Mayfield was one of the most emotive composers and performers of his age, his remarkable and emotive 'River's Invitation' being dubbed by one not unadmiring critic as: "Music to commit suicide by"!

A classy pianist, as well as a mellow-toned singer, Percy was born in Minden, Louisiana, on August 12, 1920, the son of a singer father and a dancer mother.

Leaving home to hobo through the Midwest and West, he had settled in Los Angeles by 1947 when he made his first discs for Supreme. Coming up with consistently appealing songs, usually in an intimate and laid-back mood, Percy had a distinctively mellow, soul-laden blues style which made his releases on Specialty, Cash, Atlantic and other labels steady sellers if not major hits. Percy died on August 11, 1984.

LITTLE MILTON

One-time winner of a major "Battle of the Blues" showdown against Bobby Bland and B. B. King, Little Milton Campbell was long overlooked by blues purists, partly because his stylings seemed an amalgam of what Bland and King had done first, partly because much of his material for Chess veered towards soul music. Nearly three decades later, few could deny the claim to recognition among the greats for a man whose talents are equally divided between songwriting, guitar-playing and singing.

Like King and Bland, Milton had been discovered in Memphis by Ike Turner, who in 1953 recorded the youngster—who was born at Inverness, Mississippi, on September 7, 1934—for Sam Phillips's Sun label. Following Ike Turner to St Louis, Milton used that city as his base and recorded for Bobbin before moving to Chicago and spending a highly successful period from 1961 to 1969 with Chess's Checker subsidiary.

Moving his recording base back to Memphis, Milton found even greater success with Stax, his appearance singing 'Walking The Backstreets And Crying' being a highlight of the *Wattstax* movie. Since Stax's demise, Milton has cut a number of classy albums for Malaco through to the Nineties.

ROY MILTON

A true pioneer of the commercial R&B idiom, drummer and bandleader Roy Milton was born on July 31, 1907, in Wynnewood, Oklahoma, and grew up in nearby Tulsa where he sang in the church choir and played in his high school brass band.

After a football scholarship at the University of Texas, Roy worked with the Ernie Fields Band in Tulsa before moving to California and starting his own Roy Milton and the Solid Senders outfit. The band appeared

Percy Mayfield wrote hits for Ray Charles as well as enjoying his own success as a recording star.

in the *47th Street Jive, Hey Lawdy Mama* and *Ride On Ride On* 1940s movie shorts and, already successful as a nightclub owner, Roy formed his own Milton label to record them.

Roy and his cohorts moved on to bigger things with Specialty and King, logging a run of R&B charters through the Fifties. By the Seventies, his uptown style was somewhat *passé* but he found a slot with the Johnny Otis Revue and featured on the Monterey Jazz Festival.

CHARLIE MUSSELWHITE

Born to a white mandolin-maker and a mother of Choctaw Indian descent at Koskiusko, Mississippi, on January 31, 1944, Charlie Musselwhite has earned lasting respect right across the blues community, being highly rated by both black musicians and white record collectors as one of the finest exponents of Chicago-style harmonica playing.

Raised in Memphis, he moved to Chicago in 1962 and gained early experience sitting in with Robert Nighthawk, Homesick James, J. B. Hutto and others at the Hideaway Club and other venues, besides working Maxwell Street with Johnny Young.

In 1966, Charlie appeared with the Mike Bloomfield–Barry Goldberg Blues Band on television and began recording for Vanguard, subsequent discs appearing on Blue Thumb, Arhoolie and other labels. In 1971, he backed John Lee Hooker on an ABC Dunhill album and has since supported many others of the greats.

ROBERT NIGHTHAWK

One of the originators of the bottleneck style of guitar playing, Robert Nighthawk created doom-laden, intensely brooding blues music in which the slide seemed to literally weep. His deep, impassioned and haunting vocals added to the stunning effect.

Born Robert Lee McCollum, in Helena, Arkansas, on November 30, 1909, he was a graduate of the Memphis Jug Band, with which outfit he worked from the early Twenties. Robert worked as a solo into the Thirties, often on the same bill as John Lee Hooker, at venues across the Delta. In 1937 he was in Chicago, frequently recording with Bluebird as a session player.

Between 1943 and 1947, Robert worked regularly on radio stations in Helena, Arkansas, and Clarksdale, Mississippi, returning frequently to Chicago for club and recording work before settling in the northern city for good in 1963.

Unfortunately, the great blues revival passed him by. He moved back to Arkansas and died of heart failure at Helena Hospital on November 5, 1967, before he could be rediscovered by the blues buffs.

JOHNNY OTIS

The son of Greek immigrants named Veliotes, the extrovert Johnny Otis was born on December 28, 1921, at Vallejo, California, and became a seminal figure in the development of West Coast black music through the Fifties and Sixties.

Though a talented drummer and vibes player, it was as a bandleader, record producer and talent-spotter that Johnny made his major contribution.

After an initial hit with 'Harlem Nocturne' in 1946, he opened the Barrelhouse Club in Los Angeles, in partnership with Bardu Ali, as a showcase for local talent. Soon Johnny was taking his all-star Revue out on the road, introducing audiences to such discoveries as Little Esther Phillips and Etta James, besides playing a role in the early careers of Little Willie John, Hank Ballard and Jackie Wilson and producing Johnny Ace and Little Richard for Don Robey's Peacock label.

'Willie And The Hand Jive' gave Johnny Otis a big hit of his own in 1958 and just over a decade later he turned to pure blues for the highly acclaimed *Cold Shot* album, which featured his guitar-playing son Shuggie and served to spread his fame far beyond the black ghetto, winning rock media acclaim.

Launched in 1974, Johnny's own Blues Spectrum label featured such old-time greats as Joe Turner, Pee Wee Crayton, Joe Liggins and Charles Brown. In ensuing years Johnny has continued to foster the music he loves.

LITTLE JUNIOR PARKER

Herman "Little Junior" Parker was born in blues-rich Clarksdale, Mississippi, on March 27, 1932. He served his musical apprenticeship as a harmonica player in Clarksdale and West Memphis clubs, jamming alongside Sonny Boy Williamson (Rice Miller), Howlin' Wolf and other soon-to-be greats.

Into the early Fifties, he worked the Deep South as a regular member of Howlin' Wolf's band, taking it over when the leader moved to Chicago and renaming it the Blue Flames. He also worked as an occasional member of the seminal Beale Streeters, alongside Roscoe Gordon, Johnny Ace, Billy Duncan, Earl Forrest and Bobby Bland.

Following Ace's death playing Russian roulette, on New Year's Eve 1954, Junior and Bobby Bland joined forces, taking over Ace's band and touring together as the Blues Consolidated package through till 1961. Like Bland, Junior was signed to Don Robey's Duke label, scoring with such powerhouse hits as 'The Bare Foot Rock' and 'Driving Wheel' and recording later for Minit and Blue Rock.

Junior's formidable harmonica playing increasingly took a back seat to his patent R&B-slanted vocalizing, framed by punchy brass arrangements.

In 1971, Junior found a new direction, recording with jazz/R&B organist Jimmy McGriff but, sadly, suffered a brain tumour and died suddenly at Blue Island, Illinois, on November 18, 1971.

CHARLIE PATTON

One of the major founding figures of the Mississippi Delta blues movement, Charlie Patton was born, one of 12 children, on a farm between Edwards and Bolton in 1887. When he was 10, he went to work on Will Dockery's plantation while playing at weekend hops, often joining Tommy Johnson, Willie Brown and Dick Bankston. From the mid-Twenties Charlie hoboed through Mississippi, working in logging camps and playing at parties and on the street. In 1929, he found his way north to Richmond, Indiana, where he recorded for Paramount.

Settling down in Holly Ridge, near Indianola, Mississippi, this seminal figure spent the rest of his life working locally—both inside and outside music—apart from a trip to New York to record for Vocalion in 1934.

Charlie died at his home of a heart condition on April 28 that year and was buried in an unmarked grave—a sadly lonely end for a man whose work was a major influence on Son House, Robert Johnson, Muddy Waters and so many others.

MA RAINEY

Second only to Bessie Smith among the classic women blues singers of the Twenties and Thirties, Gertrude "Ma" Rainey was an artist whose material worked the gamut of emotions, from blinding misery to utter joyfulness.

On one song reflective, on the next she would be out-right bawdy—covering a range of material which reflected her background in vaudeville. Not purely a blues singer, Ma Rainey dabbled in jazz and was a veritable genius of the *double entendre*.

Born at Columbus, Georgia, on April 26, 1886, she died in the same town on December 22, 1939 of a heart attack. In the years between, she cut some of the most memorable records of her era.

Already singing blues as early as 1902, she teamed up with and married William "Pa" Rainey two years later and they worked as a song and dance act at tent shows and theatres across the South and Midwest.

After a short period living in Mexico, Ma returned to the USA and recorded for Paramount in 1923, soon becoming a big seller on the "race record" market.

Though she died in 1939, her influence on post-war female blues singers was to be considerable.

BONNIE RAITT

When, in 1991, John Lee Hooker scored his biggest hit in many years with the classy remake of 'In The Mood', a large part of the credit was undoubtedly due to talented white girl singer Bonnie Raitt. She not only duetted on the song with John Lee,

Can a white girl sing the blues? In Bonnie Raitt's case the answer is a definite "yes".

but contributed some remarkable guitar lines as well. A superlative songwriter and a sincere lover of the blues, Bonnie has managed to work within the idiom without suffering any of the taunts of plagiarism which are so often levelled at white blues artists.

Born in the Los Angeles suburb of Burbank on November 8, 1949, Bonnie learned guitar at 9 years of age and by 1968 was based on the East Coast, working with the Sweet Stavin' Chain Band and with John Hammond Jr. in local clubs as well as touring with country blues legends Fred McDowell, Son House and Robert Pete Williams. Signed to Warner Bros in 1971, her confidence and stature as a creative musician grew steadily over the following two decades.

LOUISIANA RED

Louisiana Red—real name Iverson Minter—had his share of troubles, starting before he was even old enough to know, his mother dying within a week of his birth. Five years later his grandmother received a telegram explaining that his father had been lynched in Kentucky by the Ku-Klux-Klan. In 1972 his brother was killed by a fruit-picking machine, as Red worked alongside, and a year later his wife died at 30 of cancer. Not only that— the bluesman claims never to have received any of the royalties from Roulette for his classic 1962 album *Lowdown Backporch Blues* and the reputedly million-selling single, 'Red's Dream'.

Born in Vicksburg, Mississippi, on March 23, 1936, and raised first in New Orleans then in Pittsburgh, Red played in a street corner trio. At 14, he saw Muddy Waters play at the Skyline Club and was allowed to jam with the master.

After army service in Korea, Red called Phil Chess in Chicago and auditioned over the phone, leading to his first recordings, under the name Rocky Fuller (his numerous other recording aliases have included Elmore James Jr., Rockin' Red and Guitar Red).

After a short stint with Muddy Waters's band, Red got married and settled in New Jersey, recording for several companies before Roulette. On returning to New Jersey from a stint back in Vicksburg, Red was rediscovered by Herb Abramson, one of the founders of Atlantic Records and by then an independent producer, and subsequently recorded for Atco, Blue Labor, Black & Blue and other labels. He has been a frequent visitor to the UK and Europe.

SPECKLED RED AND PIANO RED

Brothers Rufus and Willie Perryman, who recorded as Speckled Red and Piano Red respectively—they were albinos—were key exponents of the raucous barrelhouse boogie-woogie style of blues pianists, providing a stylistic link from ragtime to modern music.

The elder by 18 years, Rufus was born on October 23, 1892, in Monroe, Louisiana.

The family—with 16 children in all—made frequent moves between Hampton, Georgia, where Willie was born on October 19, 1911 and Detroit, Michigan, eventually settling in Atlanta in 1920.

Rufus worked extensively through the South and Midwest, including stints as pianist on trains running into New Orleans, and recorded for a variety of labels through to his death from cancer in St Louis on January 2, 1972. Willie worked as a DJ on WAOK Radio in Atlanta and also recorded prolifically—one notable outing, under his other alias of Dr Feelgood, being the jaunty little instrumental 'Peachtree Parade', featuring jazz great Kenny Burrell on guitar.

The pseudonym Piano Red has also been used by John Williams, Vernon Harris and Vance Patterson.

JIMMY REED

See separate entry in the Legends section.

JIMMY ROGERS

Though overshadowed as both a guitarist and a singer by his longtime boss Muddy Waters, the personable Jimmy Rogers played a key role in the evolution of the Chicago brand of hard-hitting amplified blues.

Jimmy was born James A. Lane at Ruleville, Mississippi, on June 3, 1924, but assumed his stepfather's name of Rogers as a child. After learning guitar around 1935 on a home-made instrument, he worked local house parties with Little Arthur Johnson and spent a year in East St Louis before migrating to Chicago in 1939.

Jimmy played with Claude Smith, Sunnyland Slim and Daddy Stovepipe before joining Muddy Waters in 1948 for a seven-year round of tours, club and concert dates and recording sessions at Chess, backing not only Waters but other artists—including Sonny Boy Williamson, Howlin' Wolf and Sunnyland Slim—on both tours and record dates.

His own releases appeared on a variety of labels. After leaving the Waters' band he continued to work busily in the USA and Europe until tailing off his musical activities in the late Seventies when he became an apartment building manager, though he has continued to play the odd date and overseas tour.

OTIS RUSH

Few urban bluesmen can match the electrifying guitar technique and supercharged vocals—often wailing into high falsetto—of Otis Rush. Yet, amazingly, it was not until 1969 that he made his first album, despite years of cutting R&B chart singles, starting off with his 'I Can't Quit You Baby' theme in the early Fifties. One of seven children, Otis was born on April 29, 1934 and moved with his family to Chicago in 1948 as part of the great mass migration from the Deep South.

Otis's early Cobra sides remain classics to this day and he also recorded for Chess and others, besides appearing throughout the Midwest on the same bills as Jimmy Reed, T-Bone Walker and Little Richard, and working through Europe with the 1966 American Folk Blues Festival package. Atlantic's Cotillion subsidiary took him to Muscle Shoals, Alabama, for that 1969 album, on which he was backed by the Fame Studio team plus such notables as Duane Allman and Mark Naftalin, with white Chicago bluesmen Nick Gravenites and Mike Bloomfield as his producers. A 1977 album for Sonet was produced by blues researcher Sam Charters, reflecting the continuing esteem in which Otis was held.

JIMMY RUSHING

The archetypal blues shouter of the Oklahoma/Kansas City school, the roly-poly Jimmy Rushing was described by Dave Brubeck as "The daddy of them all" when it came to jazz blues singers.

Born on August 26, 1902 in Oklahoma City, Jimmy learned piano playing from his uncle, Wesley Manning, who he remembers as "a blues singer with a whisky voice". Moving to Los Angeles, Jimmy worked private parties with Jelly Roll Morton before returning to his home town where he linked up with Walter Page's Blue Devils for shows throughout the South and South-west.

Jimmy fronted Bennie Moten's band from 1929 to 1935 when he joined Count Basie—an affiliation which was to last until 1950. He always came over best when supported by a high-flying horn section.

Already a big name on record in the late Thirties, Jimmy attained international status with jazz and blues audiences alike and his career flourished right through to 1971 when ill health curtailed his busy schedule. He died in New York City on June 8, 1972.

MAGIC SAM

One of the second generation of electric blues artists to migrate from Mississippi to Chicago, the classy "Magic Sam" Maghett provided a stylistic bridge back to such illustrious predecessors as Muddy Waters, Jimmy Rogers and Howlin' Wolf.

Born in Grenada, Mississippi, on February 14, 1937, Sam often played guitar in that community with Magic Slim (Morris Holt) before moving to Chicago in 1950 and attending Drake High School. After a stint with the Morning View Special gospel group, he was a member of the Homesick James Band before forming his own group in 1955 and also backing Shakey Jake.

Deserting from the army in 1960, Sam recorded for Chief, CBS and Delmark before a spell with Otis Rush's band working local clubs. He made it to England to play at the Royal Albert Hall in 1969 but died later that year on December 1 after suffering a heart attack at home.

NINA SIMONE

Though much better known as a major jazz and soul star, the enigmatic Nina Simone also cut many fine blues records. Her role as a prime mover in the black emancipation movement led to such social consciousness records as 'Old Jim Crow', 'Mississippi Goddam', a majestic version of Billie Holiday's 'Strange Fruit' and the bitingly bitter 'Backlash Blues'.

Born Euniçe Waymon in North Carolina in 1933, Nina had taught herself piano and organ as a child prodigy, being much in demand in local churches. Unlike most blues artists, she had formal musical training, first at high school in Asheville, North Carolina, thanks to the sponsorship of a kindly white lady, and then at the famed Juilliard School of Music in New York, where she was a contemporary of jazz great Miles Davis.

After her family moved to Philadelphia, Nina began working the East Coast night clubs, particularly in Atlantic City, and landed a recording deal with Bethlehem Records. She cut the million-selling 'I Loves You Porgy' for them before a productive stint with Philips, from 1964 to 1967, and an RCA contract which yielded the superb *Nina Simone Sings The Blues* album.

GUITAR SLIM

Not to be confused with Norman Green or Alexander Seward, who both also used the pseudonym Guitar Slim, the highly talented Eddie Jones was a key figure on the New Orleans scene in the early Fifties.

Born in Greenwood, Mississippi, on December 10, 1926, Eddie formed a trio with Huey "Piano" Smith, of 'Rockin' Pneumonia and the Boogie Woogie Flu' fame, to work the New Orleans clubs in the late 1940s. Going solo, he adopted the "Guitar Slim" tag and became a regular at the renowned Dew Drop Inn and other Crescent City venues, besides cutting his first tracks locally, for Imperial, in 1951.

On his return from army service in Korea, he recorded classic smokey blues sides for Specialty and from 1956 to 1958 had a productive spell with Atco, but when only 33 years old he died of pneumonia on a midwinter visit to New York. The date was February 7, 1959.

Guitar Slim's own style was rooted in those of Clarence "Gatemouth" Brown and T-Bone Walker. He was, in turn, a major influence on Ray Charles and Jimi Hendrix.

LIGHTNIN' SLIM

Married to Slim Harpo's sister, Lightnin' Slim was a fellow mainstay in the mid-Sixties of the hot Louisiana-based Excello label—though his style was more in the mainstream than the swamp blues which was the company's forte.

Born Otis Hicks on March 13, 1913 near St Louis, he was raised on farms. Unlike most blacks, his family migrated south rather than north, fetching up in St Francisville, Louisiana, when he was still a child.

Late developer Lightnin' Slim nevertheless left a rich heritage from a too-short career.

It was not until he was in his mid-thirties that Lightnin' learned to play guitar.

By 1946 he was based in Baton Rouge, working local clubs, recording for Feature and Ace in 1954 and Excello in 1955–6. After living in Detroit in the Sixties, Lightnin' returned to Louisiana to cut records again for Excello with considerable success and worked prolifically with Slim Harpo. After a recording hiatus, Excello signed him again in 1972, the sessions being produced in London by Mike Vernon, using British musicians.

Lightnin' died of cancer in Detroit, Michigan, on July 27, 1974.

MEMPHIS SLIM

One of the first blues artists to win a mass audience in Europe, Memphis Slim—real name Peter Chatman—ended his days as a resident of Paris after three decades working the blues revival scene around the world. A big, warm-voiced and lusty vocalist in the urban mould, he played in a style which harked back to an older barrel-house tradition.

Raised in his home town of Memphis, where he had been born on October 15, 1925, Slim was particularly influenced by fellow piano players Roosevelt Sykes and Speckled Red before, at 24, hitching a ride to Chicago. Big Bill Broonzy advised Slim to develop his own style and gave him a seat in his band when his previous pianist, Joe Altheimer, died.

Slim worked with many of the Chicago greats, including Sonny Boy Williamson (Rice Miller) and Willie Dixon before hitting the big time in 1959 with his Carnegie Hall and Newport Folk Festival appearances, prior to embarking on his first European tour and eventually becoming a fixture at the Les Trois Maillets Club on the Left Bank in Paris.

He died in France.

SUNNYLAND SLIM

Along with his contemporaries Otis Spann, Little Brother Montgomery and Roosevelt Sykes, the colourfully named Sunnyland Slim was a key figure in the evolution of blues piano playing during Chicago's golden age.

The product of an unhappy home—he was born in Vance, Mississippi, on September 5, 1907 and raised by a stepmother with whom he rowed constantly—Sunnyland

Slim, aka Albert Luandrew, found solace playing piano and organ in church and hanging out around the Clarksdale blues clubs on Saturday nights.

In 1924, he found a job as pianist at a little picture house in nearby Lambert, moving to Memphis soon after and making that city his base for nearly 15 years, backing Ma Rainey, Blind Blake, Blind Boy Fuller, Sonny Boy Williamson and other artists when they were in town.

In 1942, Slim moved to Chicago to work in factories and as a truck driver, while gigging at night. It was five more years before he got on to record, as "Doctor Clayton's Buddy", but he was already well known around the clubs and was to be the man who introduced Muddy Waters to Aristocrat, the label which became Chess and for which Slim also recorded.

Slim recorded regularly as a frontman and backing musician through into the Eighties.

BESSIE SMITH

See separate entry in the Legends section.

VICTORIA SPIVEY

Commended by the BMI music publishing organization in 1970 for "long and outstanding contributions to the many worlds of music", Victoria Spivey was one of the proud line of classic blues singers who set the pattern for the distaff side of black music as we know it today. As Jim O'Neal, of *Rolling Stone* magazine, saw it: "Many of her blues were grim tales of death, despair, cruelty and agony, underscored by her sombre piano and stark Texas blues moans."

One of eight children, Victoria was born on October 15, 1906 in Houston, Texas, and by her teens was working as pianist at the Lincoln Theatre in Dallas.

Meeting the likes of Blind Lemon Jefferson on the Texas club and house party scene, she first recorded for OKeh in St Louis, Missouri, in 1926, enjoying the support of top calibre musicians, including Lonnie Johnson, King Oliver, Clarence Williams and Louis Armstrong on subsequent sessions.

A varied career found her recording spasmodically, working as a tour director and starring in musical comedy, as well as running her own club for a time and, in the 1970s, her own Spivey record label. Shortly after returning from a UK visit during which she appeared in *The Devil's Music—A History Of The Blues* BBC TV documentary, Victoria died of an internal haemorrhage at a hospital in New York, the city which she had made her home for some years. The date was October 3, 1976.

ROOSEVELT SYKES

Roosevelt Sykes's working names included "the Blues Man", Dobby Bragg, Easy Papa Johnson and Willie Kelly, but he was best known by the epithet of "the Honey-dripper", a nickname he picked up at school in St Louis, where his family had moved in 1909.

Roosevelt had been born three years earlier, on January 31, 1906, at Elmar, Arkansas. After playing organ in church as a teenager, his family having moved back to Arkansas, Roosevelt left home in 1921 to work barrel-houses in West Helena and Lake Providence.

The North promised more and better paid work, so he moved back to St Louis. He cut his début 78s for OKeh in Chicago in 1929, and with that city providing most of his live work and recording opportunities, Roosevelt upped sticks again and based himself in the Windy City for the rest of his career, save a short stint down in New Orleans, a city which always had a penchant for piano players.

The Sixties and Seventies produced plenty of opportunities for him to work and record in Europe where he also had a strong following.

Many of his songs, including the powerful 'Drivin' Wheel' have become blues standards.

LITTLE JOHNNY TAYLOR

Not to be confused with the other Johnnie Taylor, who became a soul superstar for Stax before reverting to a more bluesy style, Johnny (spelt with a "y") Taylor stayed more or less faithful to the brass-laden yet restrained vein of R&B also worked by such other West Coast-based artists as Charles Brown, Percy Mayfield, Jimmy McCracklin and Lowell Fulsom.

Johnny started his career as youngest member of the famed Mighty Clouds Of Joy gospel group—hence the "Little" tag—working out of Memphis, where he had been born on February 11, 1943.

Moving to Los Angeles in the late Fifties, he recorded blues for Swingin' before hitting big with his Galaxy classic 'Part Time Love', a number also later recorded by the other Johnnie Taylor.

He went on to record for Ronn, at Muscle Shoals Sound, in Alabama, and remained one of the best, if rather neglected, blues balladeers.

KOKO TAYLOR

Along with Etta James and Sugar Pie DeSanto, Koko Taylor was part of the triumvirate of superb female singers who helped Chess remain the premier label in blues music throughout the Sixties. With her rough, tough, growling voice, she was all woman as she wailed her way through 'Wang Dang Doodle', 'Be What You Want To Be', 'Nitty Gritty' and other big hits.

A native of Memphis, Tennessee, she was born on September 28, 1935 and moved to Chicago when she was 15. Schooled in gospel music, Koko turned her talents to the blues in 1953 when she began making club appearances with Buddy Guy and Junior Wells, making her first record soon after for the USA label, accompanied by J. B. Lenoir.

Leonard and Phil Chess quickly recognized Koko's emergent talents and signed her to their Checker label, which was targeted at the more commercial end of the R&B and soul market.

After the demise of the Chess organization, Koko continued to record for other Chicago labels and remains highly active, with a run of albums on Alligator.

SONNY TERRY AND BROWNIE McGHEE

The most outstandingly successful double act in blues music, blind harmonica player Sonny Terry and crippled guitarist   Brownie

McGhee successfully carried their unique form of country blues to a mass international audience.

Sonny was born Saunders Terrell, outside Durham on the North Carolina–Georgia border, on October 24, 1911. He went blind as a result of two serious car accidents, and accompanied Blind Boy Fuller on a series of recordings in the late Thirties. When Fuller died, Sonny teamed up with Brownie McGhee (born Knoxville, Tennessee, on November 30, 1914), who made his early records under the name Blind Boy Fuller II, accompanied by Sonny.

During World War II, the pair worked the New York City folk scene with Woody Guthrie and Leadbelly.

High-profile concert appearances and recordings for a variety of record labels kept their flag flying and in 1958 they delighted British audiences with their quirky, high-pace instrumental 'Silver Fox Chase'. In latter years, they worked as solos through the Seventies. Sonny died on March 11, 1986.

BIG MAMA THORNTON

When Elvis Presley covered her 'Hound Dog' R&B hit, the big hit spotlight settled briefly on Big Mama Thornton, but while latter-day white blues audiences continued to show their appreciation of her considerable

A truly gifted duo, Sonny Terry and Brownie McGhee did much to open white audiences' ears.

talents, a repeat of such wider acclaim eluded her. Though her style was full-bodied, gutsy, even aggressive, at the same time she displayed a tremendous sensitivity in her vocals, making her one of the very best blues singers of all time. "She creates tension without harshness, excitement without strain, she can make you weep," wrote leading music critic Ralph J. Gleason.

Raised in Montgomery, Alabama, where she was born on December 11, 1926, Willie Mae "Big Mama" Thornton toured the South with Sammy Green's Hot Harlem Revue between 1941 and 1948, when she settled in Houston, working local clubs and recording for Peacock. Johnny Otis, who produced for the label at the time, made her part of his touring package and she stayed with him until 1953 when she joined a similar review headed by Johnny Ace and Junior Parker.

By the Sixties, she was working out of Los Angeles and recording for various labels, one notable session teaming her with Muddy Waters and his band while her 'Ball And Chain' provided an inspiration to the emergent blues-influenced rock star Janis Joplin.

Though she never broke clear of the confines of the blues circuit, her reputation brought her steady work across America and Europe until her death.

TOMMY TUCKER

Though his fame rests essentially on just two records—the irresistibly infectious 'Hi Heel Sneekers', which was a smash hit in 1964 and became a UK hit second time around in the late 1980s, and its follow-up, 'Long Tall Shorty'—the talents of Robert Higginbotham, or Tommy Tucker to give him his stage name, run far deeper than that and he remains a continuously popular club draw on both sides of the Atlantic.

Tommy was born in Springfield, Ohio, on March 5, 1939 and began piano playing as a child. A contender for the Golden Gloves boxing title in 1950, he started his musical career on the club circuit with bands led by Bobby Woods and Clarence La Velle and also worked with jazzman Roland Kirk before moving to New Jersey and being discovered by Herb Abramson, one of the founders of Atlantic Records.

On quitting that company following military service, Abramson took Tucker's contract with him and signed his protégé to Chess in 1964 for the two hits and a resultant superb album.

BIG JOE TURNER

Starting out as a bouncer, bartender, cook and singer at clubs in Kansas City, where he was born on May 18, 1911, Joe Turner's early work was with pianist Pete Johnson, the inspiration for his 'Roll 'Em Pete' classic.

One of the great Kansas City jazz blues shouters, Big Joe became a major star with the Bennie Moten, Count Basie, Harry James, Benny Carter and Duke Ellington big bands in the swing-crazy Thirties.

In 1951 he recorded in New Orleans with Dave Bartholomew's band, then signed with Atlantic and found a whole new direction, logging a string of R&B hits which included 'Chains Of Love', the originals of the rock 'n' roll opus 'Shake, Rattle And Roll' and of 'Sweet Sixteen', which B. B. King was later to make his own, 'Honey Hush', 'Flip, Flop And Fly', his revival of the country blues standard 'Corinne, Corinna', and 'TV Mama', recorded in Chicago featuring an unmistakable bottleneck guitar riff contributed by Elmore James.

Over the years, Big Joe recorded everything from jump blues to jazz standards and in 1970, after a decade in the relative doldrums, became a featured act on the Johnny Otis Revue. He passed away on November 23, 1985.

IKE TURNER

Though subsequently better known as the Svengali-like male half of the dynamic Ike & Tina Turner husband-and-wife duo, guitar- and piano-playing Ike Turner was a seminal figure on the Fifties blues scene.

After working as a DJ and studio musician on WROX Radio in Clarksdale, Mississippi, where he had been born on November 5, 1931, Ike formed the Kings Of Rhythm and in 1950 recorded at Sam Phillips's recently opened Sun Studio in Memphis. The initial session yielded the big hit 'Rocket 88' which, credited to its singer and writer Jackie Brenston, is held by many to be "the first true rock 'n' roll record".

Though a talented singer, Ike was content to stay largely in the background, as a producer, writer, arranger, accompanist and general hustler.

Contacted by Lester Bihari, who was setting up a Memphis office for his brothers' LA-based Modern Records, Ike became a roving talent scout, using a home tape-recorder to cut such talents as Elmore James, Houston Boines, B. B. King, Junior Parker, Roscoe Gordon and Johnny Ace at sessions in Greenville and at the Memphis YMCA. Soon he was taking acts to Chess and others as well.

Moving his base to East St Louis, in 1955 Ike recorded his *Kings Of Rhythm* for the King/Federal group.

After discovering Tina in 1958, changing her name from Anna Mae Bullock and marrying her, Ike went more into a soul/funk bag. However, tucked away on consequent Ike and Tina Turner albums over the years were a number of fine blues recordings showcasing Ike's distinctive style.

EDDIE "CLEANHEAD" VINSON

Singing from the back of his throat and using quirky phrasing, Eddie Vinson had one of the most original and distinctive vocal sounds in the blues as well as being a fine alto saxophonist. His roots were in jazz, starting off as a sideman with the Cootie Williams Orchestra, which

Raunchy sax playing and inimitable vocals made up Eddie Vinson's unique sound.

he joined in 1941, and going on to recordings with various other greats of the idiom, including most notably the classy Julian "Cannonball" Adderley.

Born in Houston, Texas, on December 18, 1917, Eddie worked locally with the Milton Larkins Band before settling in New York. Leaving Cootie Williams's organization in 1954, he returned to Houston to find employment as a music teacher, besides gigging locally and cutting a few jazz discs before his landmark recordings with Adderley for Riverside in 1962, which included the 'Back Door Blues' and 'Kidney Stew' classics.

In the late Sixties, he visited Europe with the Jay McShann Orchestra and in 1974 recorded a live album at the Montreux Jazz Festival with pick-up players who included classy British blues pianist Pete Wingfield. Eddie's "Cleanhead" nickname derived from his shaven head. He died on July 2, 1988.

T-Bone Walker

See separate entry in the Legends section.

Little Walter

Marion Walter Jacobs, born on May 1, 1930 in Marksville, Louisiana, was just 12 years old when he ran away to the big city—in his case, New Orleans. Working his way north through the mid-Forties, he appeared on the Sonny Boy Williamson (Rice Miller)-hosted *King Biscuit Time* radio show, out of Helena, Arkansas, in 1944, played East St Louis clubs in 1945, and finally arrived in Chicago in 1946. He soon fell in with the likes of Tampa Red, Big Bill Broonzy and Memphis Slim on the club scene and recorded for Ora Nelle Records before becoming part of the all-star Muddy Waters Band.

The man who defined the harmonica's role in modern blues, Little Walter was a Chicago cornerstone.

Little Walter's wailing harmonica was an important part of the hard-hitting, highly-amplified sound with which Waters was revolutionizing the blues. Logging hits of his own, notably with 'My Babe' and 'Juke', Walter's success for a short time even eclipsed that of his master.

A notoriously difficult man, Walter was an outstanding musician, almost single-handedly fashioning the stylistic approach to harmonica-playing which was to become the norm within the blues genre. Following a street fight, he died of a blood clot (coronary thrombosis) on February 15, 1968, in Chicago.

DINAH WASHINGTON

An inspiration for Aretha Franklin, Esther Phillips, Etta James and other blues-slanted soul singers, Dinah Washington was an extraordinarily gifted artist whose talents transcended the confines of blues music—for she was also a unique interpreter of jazz and pop tunes. Cast in the mould of Billie Holiday, she cut many great records between 1943 and her death in Detroit of a sleeping-pill overdose 20 years later, on December 14, 1963.

Married four times and possessed of an explosive personality, Dinah performed her music with raw emotion, wringing deep pathos and melancholy from even the most banal of lyrics.

Raised in Chicago from early childhood, she had been born Ruth Lee Jones on August 29, 1924, in Tuscaloosa, Tennessee, and was grounded in gospel music.

Dinah's singing career took off when she fronted Lionel Hampton's band on dancehall and theatre dates across America between 1943 and 1946.

With her sophisticated style, she weathered the rock 'n' roll explosion and by the early Sixties was an established figurehead of the R&B scene, having worked with both Count Basie and Duke Ellington as well as making records which were precursors of soul music and earned her billing as "Queen of the Blues".

MUDDY WATERS

See separate entry in the Legends section.

JOHNNY "GUITAR" WATSON

Though his later recordings entered the realms of soul, funk and rock, Johnny "Guitar" Watson spent his early career as a wholly authentic urban bluesman.

He had already come under the influence of the Texas school of modern blues players before moving to Los Angeles in 1950. He cut his first single, 'Highway 60', for Federal three years later, when he was still only 17 years old.

Four singles and two years on, Johnny released 'Space Guitar', an instrumental on which he used echo and reverb techniques which pre-dated Jimi Hendrix by ten years. In 1958, he wrote and recorded 'Gangster Of Love', later to become a mega-hit when talented rock star Steve Miller covered it.

Having already gained a lot of experience working as a sideman with Chuck Higgins, Joe Houston, Big Jay McNeely and others, Johnny teamed up with black rock 'n' roll veteran Larry Williams and between 1965 and 1969 they cut three LPs together, mainly in the soul music idiom, as well as the quirky 'Beatletime' novelty disc, the first UK release on Mike Vernon's Blue Horizon label.

Starting with *Ain't That A Bitch* in 1976, his albums for British label DJM showed his guitar inventiveness and vocal technique at its best, though by then the blues content was much diminished.

JOHN LEE "SONNY BOY" WILLIAMSON

Often referred to as Sonny Boy Williamson I, to avoid confusion with the other Sonny Boy Williamson (Rice Miller), who was actually older but arrived in Chicago later and was, therefore, known as Sonny Boy II, John Lee Williamson died in hospital on June 1, 1948. He had been mugged and stabbed in the head with an ice pick on leaving Chicago's Plantation Club after a show. It was a violent and tragic end for one of Chicago's most important bluesmen.

Sonny Boy Williamson II (Rice Miller) merited his tag of "the Grand Vizier", as he wove his magic sound.

He had left Jackson, Tennessee, where he had been born on March 30, 1914, to hobo across his home state and Tennessee with fellow blues players Yank Rachell and "Sleepy" John Estes through the Twenties and Thirties. Arriving in Chicago in 1934, Sonny Boy worked as a sideman in various groups and recorded for RCA's Bluebird label from 1939 to 1945.

He played with Big Bill Broonzy and often recorded with Big Joe Williams, winning acclaim as the first truly virtuoso blues harmonica player and a powerful singer, helping shape the course of the classic Chicago blues style.

SONNY BOY WILIAMSON II (RICE MILLER)

Tall, wizened and sporting a goatee beard, Sonny Boy Williamson—"the Grand Vizier of the Blues"—was a charismatic character when he appeared on British TV in the mid-Sixties and attracted hordes of teenage mod girls as well as blues addicts to his club dates, on which he was backed by local bands, notably the Cyril Davies All-Stars, Brian Auger And The Trinity and the Yardbirds, who included the young Eric Clapton. Sonny Boy wore a bowler hat and a well-cut suit—albeit styled in black and white panels. He carried his harmonicas on stage in a briefcase.

It was all a long way from his beginnings in the poverty-stricken Mississippi Delta, where he was born at Glendora on December 5, 1899 or thereabouts as Aleck (or Alex) Ford, later assuming his stepfather Jim Miller's surname and later still becoming known as Rice Miller—probably for his radio advertising work for a rice company. He had already adopted the name Sonny Boy Williamson by the time he landed his own *King Biscuit Time* radio show after early experience in juke joints and at house parties with Elmore James, Arthur Crudup, Robert Johnson, Howlin' Wolf (whose sister he married in 1937) and other acts.

Already a major name in the South thanks to his broadcasting and records for local labels, Sonny Boy hit the big time when he moved to Chicago, spending eight years, from 1955 to 1963, as a member of the Chess family of artists and becoming a mainstay of the American Folk Blues Festival, touring as far afield as Poland and Scandinavia. Unfortunately, at the very peak of his popularity, he passed away in his sleep on May 25, 1965 at his home in Helena, Arkansas. He should not be confused with John Lee "Sonny Boy" Williamson.

JIMMY WITHERSPOON

Charlie Musselwhite, one of the most respected white blues artists, said of Jimmy Witherspoon: "There are a lot of guys around who shout the blues and a lot who belt the blues, but Jimmy Witherspoon is different—he sings the blues." With his warm, mellow, dark-brown voice, "Spoon" has weathered never-ending changes in stylistic fashion and recent problems with throat cancer to remain one of blues music's most loved artists.

Though he was born at Gurdon, Arkansas, on August 8, 1923, Jimmy ran away from home at such an early age that it was on the West Coast that his musical tastes were formed. Service in the Pacific and Indian Oceans with the American merchant navy in the Second World War, during which he appeared on Armed Services Radio out of Calcutta, introduced him to even wider popular music influences.

Replacing Walter Brown with the Jay McShann band, he straddled blues and jazz, recording with Ben Webster among other notables of the latter idiom, and became a big star by the early Fifties. He was making $100,000 a year. Then came rock 'n' roll and he was lucky if he could pull $75 a gig.

Like so many blues artists, Jimmy found Europe to be a much richer hunting ground. He toured there extensively between 1964 and 1969 and became a regular winner of the *Melody Maker* poll.

In 1971 he cut an album with Eric Burdon of the Animals, and four years later enjoyed his biggest ever hit with 'Love Is A Five Letter Word', recorded, surprisingly, at Chipping Norton, in Oxfordshire.

The rich-voiced Jimmy Witherspoon straddles the blues and jazz idioms with ease.

HOWLIN' WOLF

A hulking man with a big, gruff voice, Chester Arthur Burnett worked under the aliases Big Foot and Bull Cow before hitting on the Howlin' Wolf tag.

One of six children, he was born at West Point, Mississippi, on June 10, 1910 and grew up on the Young and Myers Plantation, near Ruleville. Working all over the Delta area in the Thirties, Wolf came into regular contact with Sonny Boy Williamson (Rice Miller), Robert Johnson and others, teaming up regularly with Johnson's stepson, Robert Jr. Lockwood.

After army service in 1941–5, he returned to farming country, working as a fieldhand by day and making music by night before becoming an advertising salesman, producer and DJ with KWEM Radio in West Memphis. His first recordings for Memphis-based Sun Records were leased to Chess, with which latter label he was to achieve world renown thanks to a steady flow of momentous, brooding classics, usually produced, and sometimes written, by house producer Willie Dixon.

Based in Chicago from 1952, Howlin' Wolf quickly became a blues superstar thanks to his dark, brooding and immensely rich voice, harmonica and guitar work.

A hero of the rock stars, he recorded for the Rolling Stones label in 1971 with an album featuring Eric Clapton, Stevie Winwood, Bill Wyman, Charlie Watts and other luminaries. Falling victim to cancer, he died on January 10, 1976 in hospital at Hine, Illinois.

A giant in every way, Howlin' Wolf married the Delta mood with Chicago's highly amplified approach.

95

JUNIOR WELLS

One of the key figures in developing the amplified Chicago style of harmonica playing, Junior Wells was the major influence on such white practitioners as Paul Butterfield, Rod Piazza and Charlie Musselwhite. Hard-rocking, tight small-combo Chicago blues has been his forte, leading to a steady output of albums and live dates, often working with Buddy and Phil Guy.

A native of Memphis, where he was born on December 9, 1934, Amos "Junior" Wells, grew up across the river in West Memphis, Arkansas, moving to Chicago in 1941. Together with Dave and Louis Myers, he formed the Little Boys group in 1948, quickly changing the name to first the Three Deuces then the Three Aces, making a number of fine records.

By 1952, Junior had replaced Little Walter in Muddy Waters's band, reforming the Three Aces in 1956 before teaming up with Buddy Guy, with whom he has toured and recorded off and on ever since.

A forceful singer and high-energy mouth harp player, Junior Wells has made frequent visits to Europe over the past 30 years.

JOHNNY WINTER

A white, partially blind albino Texan, Johnny Winter has not only proved to be a remarkably good exponent of blues guitar playing, he has also made a notable contribution towards bringing due recognition to the black masters who had created the style in the first place, especially through his Blue Sky label, launched in the Seventies, which provided a sympathetic outlet for Muddy Waters, among others.

Johnny was born in Leland, Mississippi, on February 23, 1944 but lived in Beaumont, Texas, from an early age, forming Johnny And The Jammers in 1959 and winning local talent contests.

With a line-up including his brother Edgar, the Johnny Winter Band was signed by Columbia in 1969 for a massive advance and to the accompaniment of almost overwhelming hype. Though his bluesy albums for the label sold well, his style did not transfer well to the large concert auditorium, being more suited to intimate clubs.

After the fuss died down, Johnny forgot about rock superstardom and returned to what he did best—playing highly authentic hard rocking electric blues, his guitar skills being matched by Rory Gallagher, Duane Allman and very few others among white blues guitar players.

Harmonica hero Junior Wells has rocked the blues for three decades.

BOBBY BLAND

Blues With a Feeling

Singer/Songwriter
Born: June 27, 1930,
Rosemark, Tennessee, USA

*I*N TERMS OF RECORD SALES ALONE, BOBBY "BLUE" BLAND
WARRANTS INCLUSION IN ANY LIST OF BLUES LEGENDS—FOR NO OTHER
ARTIST IN THE IDIOM HAS CHARTED AS MANY TIMES, NOT MERELY IN THE
R&B LISTINGS BUT IN THE POP RATINGS TOO. MOREOVER, NOT ONLY
HAS BLAND EXERTED HUGE COMMERCIAL APPEAL—HE HAS SHOWN
REMARKABLE ARTISTRY AS WELL AND KNOWS FEW PEERS IN THAT SHAD-
OWY AREA WHERE BLUES MUSIC MERGES WITH SOUL.

Not the best looking of men, Bobby's rich, warm yet guttural-edged voice
could melt the heart of any woman, making him the star *par excellence* of the
"Chittlin' Circuit" in America's black neighbourhoods.

He was born Robert Calvin Bland in the small cotton town of Rosemark,
Tennessee, near Memphis, on June 27, 1930 and had his early grounding in
gospel music, as well as learning to play guitar at the early age of 5.

In 1947, he moved to Memphis and got a job as a garage mechanic, spending his weekends singing with gospel groups and eventually forming the
Miniatures to work in that idiom. After a spell working as chauffeur and valet
to B. B. King, Bland became part of the loose-knit and now near-legendary

Beale Streeters, an outfit led by saxophonist Billy Duncan, which also featured Johnny Ace—soon to become America's biggest R&B star—on piano, and Earl Forrest, with Roscoe Gordon and Bobby sharing vocal chores and B. B. King occasionally sitting in on guitar.

When Ike Turner came into town to record Gordon, King and other talents, they insisted he give some time to their young protégé. On these early sides, Bland was supported by Little Junior Parker, another occasional Beale Streeter.

Those early sides were licensed to Chess in Chicago and Modern out on the West Coast but Bobby was not on hand to promote them, having been drafted into the US Army. While in the forces, Bobby was spotted and signed up at a Houston, Texas, talent show by local entrepreneur Don Robey, who had just bought the Memphis-based Duke label from DJ James Mattis.

On Christmas Eve 1963, Johnny Ace, who had also signed with Robey, died playing Russian Roulette backstage at the City Auditorium in Houston. Joe Scott, who had been Ace's musical director, was now put on Bobby Bland's case and the combination proved magic. In the spring of 1955, a year after his discharge, 'It's My Life Baby' became Bland's first hit, his career really taking off two years later with the potent 'Farther On Up The Road', featuring Pat Hare's inspired guitar work.

But if Hare was good, Wayne Bennett—cited by no less authorities than B. B. King and Steve Cropper as "the finest blues guitarist ever"—was even better and, added to the horn-laden Bill Harvey big band and Scott's innovative arrangements, the framework was complete for Bobby "Blue" Bland's finest records. 'Cry, Cry, Cry', 'I Pity The Fool', 'Ain't Nothin' You Can Do', 'Call On Me', 'Ain't Doin' Too Bad' and dozens more were gems of the uptown blues style.

Despite the inexorable rise of James Brown and the stars of Stax, Atlantic and Motown, Bobby remained at the pinnacle of black music, but where his peers won a huge white audience, Bobby's appeal remained confined to the ghetto. His lack of business acumen, the caution which stopped him from flying—and thus from visiting Europe—and a battle with alcoholism did not help, nor did his rather forbidding appearance and ungainly stage manner.

Things changed, though, in 1973. Until that point, Bobby had spent almost his entire career under Don Robey's aegis. When Robey sold his Duke/Peacock empire to the mighty ABC/Dunhill combine, Bobby Bland went with the package.

The new affiliation brought a new direction and a change of scene. Bobby started working out of the West Coast, with new producers and arrangers. He cut well-received duo albums with his old friend B. B. King and, at last, in the Eighties, made it to Europe.

Most recently, Bobby Bland has recorded for the Birmingham, Alabama-based Malaco label, which affiliation has taken him back from the sophisticated West Coast musical settings of the MCA era to a more downhome style which amply suits his remarkable voice.

BIG BILL BROONZY

Taking Blues to the World

Singer/Songwriter/Guitarist
Born: June 26, 1893, Scott, Mississippi, USA
Died: August 15, 1958, Chicago, USA

*B*IG BILL BROONZY'S ROLE IN THE DEVELOPMENT OF THE BLUES HAS LONG BEEN THE SUBJECT OF HEATED DEBATE. WHILE HIS INBRED TALENT FOR SELF-PROMOTION MAY HAVE OVERINFLATED HIS REPUTATION AS AN INNOVATOR AND, AT THE SAME TIME, ALIENATED PURISTS— WHO BELIEVED HE HAD SOLD HIS SOUL FOR THE SAKE OF CATCHING WHITE FOLK MUSIC AUDIENCES—THERE IS NO DOUBT THAT HE WAS A MAJOR FIGURE, NOT ONLY FOR HIS OWN MUSIC BUT FOR THE GUIDING HAND WHICH HE GAVE TO OTHERS.

Muddy Waters, Little Walter Jacobs, John Sellers and Memphis Slim were among those who acknowledged the debt.

In 'Big Bill Blues', Broonzy stated: "I don't want the old blues to die. If they do then I'll be dead too, because that's the only kind I can play and sing and I love the old style." To some, that comment marked him as a charlatan because he had arrived in Chicago as far back as 1920 and had long been working in an urban blues band setting before astutely switching back to an old-fashioned rural, acoustic, one-man blues style to catch the white beatnik/folknik audience.

Certainly, his claim to be "the last of the great country blues singers" was ludicrous, especially with such redoubtable talents as Lonnie Johnson, Big Joe Williams and Sleepy John Estes still doing the rounds, but who could blame him for cashing in—for till then, despite his depth of artistry, he had never been able to support himself full-time from music, being forced to scuffle along by day as a cook, a railroad car attendant, a moulder, a porter and a piano-mover.

Nobody could argue with the credentials of his rural background. Both his parents had been born into slavery on Southern plantations. One of 17 children, William Lee Conley Broonzy first saw light of day on June 26, 1893, moving as a child from his birthplace of Scott, Mississippi, to Pine Bluff, Arkansas.

He worked as a sharecropper and an itinerant preacher. At country hops he played violin to segregated audiences who shared the same music but ate their picnics at different ends of the field. After 2 years' army service, Broonzy moved

Big Bill Broonzy listens as British trad jazzman
Humphrey Lyttelton brings an odd slant to his material.

sold mainly in the urban ghettos, and solo country blues for Verve, MGV and other companies or entated towards white audiences.

Broonzy's sessions often featured Memphis Slim and Broonzy returned the compliment, backing Slim, his own half-brother Washboard Sam, and Sonny Boy Williamson I.

By 1951, Broonzy's renown had spread worldwide, leading to concert appearances in Europe, South America, Africa and Australia. He was a particular favourite in both Denmark and France, where he made numerous recordings and had long stints working local clubs. His songs became standard fodder on the folk circuit where his name was regularly bandied about by such trendsetters as Pete Seeger.

Like Seeger, Broonzy is now remembered not so much for his own music as for his role in popularizing his chosen music forms to a truly international audience.

Broonzy died of cancer in Chicago on August 15, 1958.

to Chicago where he took guitar lessons from Papa Charlie Jackson. "My own pa had told me to choose between the church and them blues. He said the two didn't mix. I chose the blues," he recalled.

Jackson took his protégé to Paramount, where he himself recorded, but A&R man Mayo Williams turned Broonzy down time and again until finally giving him a shot with 'Big Bill Blues', in 1927.

It was not until RCA began issuing Broonzy's records on their Bluebird label that he began to be noticed. In 1939 John Hammond booked him on his *Spirituals To Swing* show at New York's Carnegie Hall and Broonzy was amazed to find that the predominantly white audience wanted to hear acoustic sharecropper songs rather than the hard urban Chicago blues which was by then his style.

Broonzy sensibly went for both audiences over the following decade, cutting hard-rocking records for labels like Chess and Mercury, which

JOHN LEE HOOKER

Master of the Boogie

Singer/Songwriter/Guitarist
Born: August 22, 1917, Clarksdale, Mississippi, USA

*A*FTER YEARS AS ONE OF THE MOST CONSISTENTLY POPULAR BLUES ARTISTS AMONG AFICIONADOS, JOHN LEE HOOKER SUDDENLY CAME GOOD IN THE NINETIES WITH A SERIES OF RECORD-INGS WHICH MADE HIM A POPULAR MUSIC SUPERSTAR.

The powerful *The Healer* album—which featured a remake of his early 'In The Mood' hit, recorded as a duet with Bonnie Raitt—and follow-up *Mr Lucky* set shook the charts apart. Then came the use of a re-recording of his classic 'Boom Boom' in a popular TV commercial—all of which introduced his intense, half-mumbled style to a mass audience spanning all age groups and racial divides. Not that Hooker had been starved of success previously—his first million-seller was as long ago as 1949.

Born in the Delta country at Clarksdale, Mississippi, on August 22, 1917, Hooker was one of 11 children. To the dismay of his deeply religious father, he learned the rudiments of blues guitar playing from Tony Hollins, his elder sister's boyfriend. After his mother's divorce, John Lee began playing music with his new stepfather,

William Moore, working dances and Saturday night fish-fries during the late Twenties. At 14, he left home for Memphis, working with Robert Nighthawk and others for a while before moving north to Cincinnati. He lived there between 1933 and 1943, playing with gospel outfits like the Big Six, the Delta Big Four and the Fairfield Four.

Shifting base to Detroit, he worked in the steel mills, formed his own band and, from the late Forties, began recording regularly, initially for the Los Angeles-based Modern label, logging a million-seller with 'Boogie Chillun' from his first sessions, and then prolifically through the early Fifties for a wide range of labels including King, Regent, Savoy, Staff, Gone, Chance, Chess, De Luxe, Gotham and Specialty, using such pseudonyms as Birmingham Sam, John Lee Booker, John Lee Cooker, Boogie Man, Delta John, Johnny Lee, Texas Slim and Johnny Williams.

John Lee gave them whatever they wanted, switching easily from a brash, intense urban style back to the haunting, often solo, mood of the Delta from where he had come. This chameleon-like quality in his work served him well, enabling him to benefit from both the folkblues revival of the late Fifties and the R&B boom of the early Sixties.

A popular music superstar into the Nineties, the great John Lee Hooker logged his first million-seller way back in the late 1940s.

John Lee's influence was enormous. Emergent rock stars Stevie Winwood, Pete Townshend, Van Morrison and Eric Burdon and white blues players John Mayall and Johnny Winter all professed their admiration and several got to play with him.

John Lee's records for Vee Jay and notably such cuts as 'Onions', 'Dimples' and 'Boom Boom'—the latter two taking him into the UK pop charts—were, for many, the zenith of his career but, in fact, he was to cut many more fine sides. One especially potent offering was the quirky *Free Beer And Chicken* album which featured—uncredited—many of the finest rock musicians of the day, including Joe Cocker, and used the weird time changes, irregular modal structures and meditative, incantatory intimacy which have become something of a hallmark of John Lee's work.

By 1970, encouraged by white blues band Canned Heat, "the Boogie Man" had relocated to the Bay Area of Northern California, carrying out a gruelling round of worldwide concerts, occasionally working with

his cousin Earl Hooker as well as other blues greats, and recording sessions for an ever-growing roster of labels including Riverside, Stax, Liberty, ABC, Bluesway and Jazz.

In 1990, at the age of 69, John Lee found new impetus with *The Healer* and *Mr Lucky*, which gained him two entries in the *Guinness Book of Records*—for the highest UK chart position ever attained by a blues album and as the oldest performer ever to reach the Top 5.

He collaborated with old friend Miles Davis on the score for Dennis Hopper's *The Hot Spot* movie, played the title role in Pete Townshend's rock opera *The Iron Man*, was honoured by an all-star tribute concert at Madison Square Gardens, which featured Willie Dixon and Charlie Musselwhite among others, and virtually turned Eric Clapton and the Rolling Stones into his backing band when he guested on a Stones tour.

Reaching back to the music's earliest traditions, there is no blues deeper than John Lee's, yet paradoxically, none also with a more wide-ranging commercial appeal.

ELMORE JAMES

Slide Guitar Genius

Singer/Songwriter/Guitarist
Born: January 27, 1918, Richland, Mississippi, USA
Died: May 23, 1963, Chicago, USA

𝒯HE MOST COPIED GUITAR SOUND IN THE BLUES HAS TO BE ELMORE JAMES'S BOTTLENECK RIFF FROM 'DUST MY BROOM'—HE HIMSELF REPRODUCED IT ON MANY OF HIS OTHER RECORDINGS, AND COUNTLESS OTHERS HAVE FOLLOWED SUIT. FROM HIS OWN CONTEMPORARIES TO FLEETWOOD MAC—THEY'VE ALL UTILIZED IT AT SOME TIME OR OTHER.

Yet, despite its familiarity, it is a sound so electrifying that it defies being tagged as a cliché. It was a sound Elmore developed from early experience at the age of 12 running a broken bottleneck down a wire strung to the side of his family's shack in deepest Mississippi.

Born on January 27, 1918 at Richland, near Durrant, on the Illinois Central Railroad midway between Jackson and Greenwood, he was the illegitimate son of Leola Brooks, taking the surname of his stepfather Joe Willie James.

At 16, Elmore owned a real guitar and started working dances and country suppers, barrelhouses and juke joints, coming into contact and playing with the likes of Hound Dog Taylor, Arthur "Big Boy" Crudup, Sonny Boy Williamson (Rice Miller), James and Johnny Shines and Robert Johnson's stepson, Robert Jr. Lockwood, while distilling his highly individual style from the influences of Robert Johnson, Kokomo Arnold and Robert Nighthawk.

During the late Thirties, it was Sonny Boy who encouraged him to travel further afield, working throughout the South.

War service with the US Navy in Guam from 1943 to 1945 was followed by moves, first to Belzoni, then to Memphis, then to Jackson, where he ran a small radio repair shop. He was a regular guest on Sonny Boy's *King Biscuit Time* radio show in Helena, Arkansas, and worked with his cousin, Homesick James, and Eddie Taylor.

In 1951, Lilian McMurry, wife of a local furniture dealer, set up the Diamond Recording Company and began recording local talent, James débuting with Luther Huff, Willie Love and Sonny Boy on the subsidiary Trumpet label. Within a year, 'Dust My Broom'—recorded, he claimed, without his knowledge, and with a flipside on which he didn't even appear—had made the nationwide R&B Top 10 listings and Elmore had left for Chicago, as the result, he said, of "girl trouble".

Signing to the Bihari brothers' Meteor company in December 1952,

Elmore James developed the most copied guitar riff of them all.
....

he cut his first Chicago sessions with the Little Johnny Jones Band—featuring Jones on piano and the talented J. T. Brown on saxophone—an association which was to last for three years. For his début, he reworked 'Dust My Broom' as 'I Believe' and made the R&B best-sellers again. Switched to the subsidiary Flair label, Elmore also recorded sides for Checker with his own Broomdusters band, and enjoyed his golden years from 1953 to 1956, before the rock 'n' roll explosion stole young black audiences from the blues. He recorded for Chief in 1957, but though the records sold well enough for the bigger Vee Jay company to reissue them, Elmore was by then already back in Jackson, working as a DJ.

He returned to Chicago in 1959. His lone release for Chess was a commercial flop but was musically one of his best, the endless repetitions of 'Dust My Broom' having been swapped for a slower, more intense style which was to mark many of his subsequent recordings for Bobby Robinson's New York-based Fire label, through to 1962, with the haunting 'The Sky Is Crying' as its masterwork. Sales of these later recordings were enough to encourage Elmore to go out on the road again but union troubles and ill-health with asthma brought his career to a halt and he returned to Jackson and obscurity.

With a new, white, international audience rapidly building for the blues, popular Chicago DJ Big Bill Hill was resolved to help Elmore make a big come-back and, in the spring of 1963, he sorted out the union problem, arranged live appearances and a recording date for the USA label and sent Elmore the fare to return north.

Sadly, Elmore died of a heart attack at Homesick James's house shortly after arriving in Chicago. The date was May 23, 1963. Elmore had never made his fortune and had little to leave his wife and three children but bequeathed the rest of us a rich legacy of consistently brilliant, atmosphere-charged recordings.

ROBERT JOHNSON

King of the Delta Blues

Singer/Songwriter/Guitarist
Born: *circa* 1912, Hazlehurst, Mississippi, USA
Died: August 16, 1938, near Greenwood, Mississippi, USA

ROBERT JOHNSON CUT ONLY 29 SIDES DURING WHAT WAS A VERY BRIEF CAREER. HE DIED A VIOLENT DEATH—THE VICTIM OF A POISONING—AT THE AGE OF JUST 26, YET THE LEGACY HE LEFT HAS BEEN ENORMOUS. THOSE EERIE, SCRATCHY, ALMOST ETHEREAL OLD RECORDINGS OF HIS ECHO DOWN THE YEARS AND HAVE BEEN THE ROOT SOURCE FOR A LEGION OF BLUES AND ROCK MUSICIANS—FROM ELMORE JAMES AND MUDDY WATERS TO ERIC CLAPTON AND JIMI HENDRIX.

Since dubbed "the King of the Delta Blues Singers", Johnson remains a shadowy, enigmatic figure, despite recent intensive research into his life which led to a John Hammond Jr. television documentary which unveiled as many new questions as it answered old ones.

Though his father was one Charles Dodds, Robert's mother was living with Noah Johnson when the baby arrived (as one of at least 10 children born to her) and he took Johnson's name. His birthdate is believed to have been sometime around 1912. Soon after, the family moved from Hazlehurst, Mississippi, to the Leatherman Plantation in nearby Commerce, where Robert was raised by a new stepfather, Robert "Dusty" Saunders.

A wild, restless child, Robert, already adept on harmonica, left home as a teenager to work the juke joints with Son House, who was the major influence on his evolving guitar style—often using a bottleneck to create a strangely haunting sound. Hoboing his way round the country—throughout the Deep South and as far afield as Texas, New York and west to the Dakotas—Robert worked everything from street corners and country lumber camps to big city speakeasies.

It was in Texas that his five recording sessions took place—three for Vocalion, held in a San Antonio hotel room on November 23, 26 and 27, 1936, and two for American Record Corporation, at a makeshift studio in the back of a Dallas office building on the weekend of June 19 and 20, 1937. The probably apocryphal story goes that a group of Mexican musicians were witnesses to the first session and that Robert was so shy of playing in front of them that he turned his face to the wall. But he certainly was not shy when it came to women, and his liking for

them—and for hard drink—was regularly to land him in trouble and eventually to lead to his death.

Don Law, who produced the sessions for ARC, remembered the bluesman as slim, good looking, of medium height, with beautiful slender hands and a remarkable ability to project his songs.

While he appeared as far north as Detroit, Michigan, in 1937, on the *Elder Moten Hour* radio show, Robert Johnson's regular stomping ground was around the Greenwood area of Mississippi where he worked at juke joints and parties with Honeyboy Edwards, Sonny Boy Williamson (Rice Miller) and Howlin' Wolf.

Though married to Esther Lockwood—his stepson, Robert Jr. Lockwood also became a renowned blues artist—Robert revelled in his role as a womanizer and hellraiser; indeed, he played hard on the old folk superstition that bluesmen had sold their souls to the devil: "You may bury my body down by the highway side/So my old evil spirit can get on a Greyhound bus and ride" ('Me And The Devil Blues').

Where, exactly, he is buried remains in dispute—memorials have been erected in at least two different graveyards—but it is now known that he died of poisoning (not stabbing as was once rumoured), his drinks having been laced by a jealous man during a show at the Three Forks Store juke joint, outside Greenwood on August 16, 1938.

A contract for him to appear on John Hammond's monumental *Spirituals To Swing* concert bill at New York's prestigious Carnegie Hall was already on its way at the time and there is little doubt that Robert Johnson had many more fine recordings in him and would have gone on to make an even more monumental contribution to the blues—if his wild life hadn't got him first.

He was certainly the most innovative artist of his day—and probably the most influential ever. Compositions like 'I Believe I'll Dust My Broom', 'Sweet Home Chicago', 'Crossroads Blues', 'Terraplane Blues' and 'Love In Vain' have become major blues anthems the world over.

B. B. KING

Blues You Can Use

Singer/Songwriter/Guitarist
Born: September 16, 1925, Itta Bena, near Indianola,
Mississippi, USA

KING BY NAME, KING BY NATURE, B.B. OF THAT ILK IS A
TRUE COLOSSUS OF BLUES MUSIC, HIS TALENT STILL HOLDING STRONG IN
THE NINETIES AFTER A GRUELLING NEAR HALF-CENTURY OF PLAYING 300
OR MORE SHOWS A YEAR AND RECORDING PRODIGIOUSLY.

Born Riley B. King on September 16, 1925 at Itta Bena, just outside Indianola, Mississippi, to plantation workers and part-time gospel singers Albert King and Nora Ella Pully, he later on took the B.B. epithet from his early show-business nickname of "Blues Boy", a tag given him by Memphis DJ Don Kearn.

His parents separated when he was 3 and he moved with his mother to Kilmichael, where he was largely looked after by the Cotledges, a white family who employed him as a farmhand. Working the land as a tractor driver earned him deferment of military service during the war after a few months of basic training and he was able to develop his craft as a musician, firstly in gospel music then, after moving to Memphis in 1946, in the blues.

Sometime during 1949, Sonny Boy Williamson (Rice Miller) gave the young musician a break with a 10-minute slot on the Hadicol-sponsored show he hosted on KWEM Radio out of West Memphis, Arkansas, on the other side of the broad Mississippi river. Soon, B.B. had his own radio show on WDIA, beamed from Memphis, with the billing "Riley King, the Blues Boy From Beale Street" which contracted to "Beale Street Blues Boy", then "Blues Boy" and finally "B.B.".

Besides DJing, he was playing club dates and recorded 'Miss Martha King' for Bullet, with backings from the Tuff Green Band. His guitar style was heavily influenced by jazzman Charlie Christian and by T-Bone Walker, while his vocals were honed alongside those of Johnny Ace, Roscoe Gordon and his own chauffeur/valet Bobby "Blue" Bland who were in the loose-knit Beale Streeters aggregation with which he also sometimes appeared.

Ike Turner, then a session man and talent scout, but later to win fame as one half of Ike And Tina Turner, brought B.B. to the attention of the Bihari brothers, Joe and Jules, who ran the RPM, Modern and Kent labels out of Los Angeles and were about to set up a Memphis office under their brother Saul. Recorded in a hired room at the Memphis YMCA in May 1949 and issued on RPM, 'Three O'Clock

Blues'—a cover of a Lowell Fulsom song—featured Ike Turner on piano, Willie Mitchell on trumpet and Hank Crawford on alto sax. It sold more than a million copies, staying at Number 1 on the American R&B charts for 18 weeks and launching B. B. King nationally.

By 1955, he had already enjoyed seven big hits and bought a converted bus to tour the country, starting to record regularly in Los Angeles with producer Maxwell Davis. Classic numbers like 'Sweet Little Angel', 'Sweet Sixteen', 'Eyesight To The Blind', 'Woke Up This Morning' and 'Rock Me Baby' kept the man's flag flying high.

B.B.'s 11-year stint with RPM ended in 1961 when he landed a major deal with ABC, continuing the hits with numbers like 'Don't Answer The Door' and 'Lucille', the latter dedicated to his Gibson guitar, which he calls by that name.

The classic 1964 *Live At The Regal* set, recorded in Chicago, revealed the depth of B.B.'s continuing appeal to black audiences at a time when they generally regarded the blues as somewhat passé, but he was now also reaching out to grab a whole new white audience.

He had already experimented with the use of string accompaniments and in 1969 came up with the haunting 'The Thrill Is Gone', which became a major cross-over hit. A year later, he was recording with white rock musicians Carole King, Joe Walsh and Leon Russell for the *Indianola Mississippi Seeds* set.

Under the astute guidance of manager Sidney Seidenberg, B.B. worked all the options, with recordings aimed at capturing soul, rock and even MOR audiences, as well as the blues buffs. He recorded at Abbey Road, in London, with such guests as Ringo Starr, Steve Marriott and Klaus Voorman, live at Cook County Jail and the University of Mississippi, with the Crusaders jazz funk band and with Stevie Wonder and, most notably, with his old friend from Memphis days, Bobby "Blue" Bland.

B. B. King and his guitar Lucille—one of the greatest partnerships in modern music.

109

JIMMY REED

Big Boss Man

Singer/Songwriter/Guitarist/Harmonica player
Born: September 6, 1925, near Dunleith, Mississippi, USA
Died: August 29, 1976, Oakland, USA

*I*N MANY WAYS THE JAMES BROWN OF THE BLUES, JIMMY REED SEEMED TO HAVE JUST A COUPLE OF TUNES TO HIS NAME BUT MANAGED TO REMAKE, REMOULD AND REJUVENATE THEM TO CREATE A HIGHLY ATTRACTIVE AND DISTINCTIVE, IF IN MANY WAYS SIMPLISTIC, SLANT ON THE BLUES IDIOM.

If he plagiarized his own songs, then the emergent white R&B bands of the early Sixties literally plundered Jimmy's material—the Rolling Stones, for example, reworking 'Shame, Shame, Shame' as 'Little By Little' while 'Big Boss Man', 'You Got Me Dizzy' and 'You Got Me Running' became standard fodder for enthusiastic young groups across the UK.

Unreliable, often the worst for drink, plagued by ill health, Jimmy Reed was the bane of record producers and concert promoters alike, but few failed to appreciate the creativity of a man who, in the words of Jim O'Neal, writing in *Living Blues* magazine, "composed, sang and played an enormously influential style of blues based on simplicity and a warm, relaxed sort of charm".

One of ten children, Mathis James "Jimmy" Reed was born on September 6, 1925 to Joseph Reed and Virginia Ross, who were sharecroppers on Mr Johnny Collier's plantation, near Dunleith, Mississippi. From the age of 7,

Jimmy was raised alongside slightly older Eddie "Playboy" Taylor, who taught him guitar. In 1939, he dropped out of school to work as a farmhand and soon after moved to Meltonia where he sang in the Pilgrim Rest Baptist Church choir.

Though rooted in the Delta, Reed's emergent laid-back, almost lazy, style had more in common with the Louisiana swamp blues of Slim Harpo, Lazy Lester, Silas Hogan and others, relying on a repetitive rhythm and simple accompaniment behind his guitar riffs and basic but effective harmonica playing.

He first moved to Chicago in 1940 and then spent 1943–5 in the US Navy, returning to Dunleith for just a year before moving north to the industrial city of Gary, Indiana, in 1948, where he worked the streets and clubs with John Brim and Joe "Jody" Duncan before, in 1949, setting up a regular band, with his old sidekick Eddie Taylor.

Jimmy made his first recordings for the Chance and Parrot labels in Chicago during 1953 and later that year got his first big break when he

Mod icon Jimmy Reed was hero to a generation of hip British kids.

started a 12-year association with the highly active and promotionally aggressive Vee Jay label, which had just been formed by Vivian Carter and James Bracken as one of the first important black-owned companies.

In later years, it was the money Vee Jay earned through its two major white acts—the Four Seasons and the Beatles—which provided the funding needed to keep Jimmy's career in high profile and made him, along with labelmate John Lee Hooker, one of the prime beneficiaries of the European R&B explosion. Club dates and ITV's popular *Ready, Steady, Go* music show brought Jimmy to Britain in 1963 for a successful first visit which made him a hero of the new mod movement.

The late Sixties blues boom should also have helped his fortunes but label changes—with rather mediocre sides for Vivid, Exodus, Bluesway Roker and Blues On Blues—didn't work out and recurrent ill-health from epilepsy, which had blighted him since 1957, meant forced inactivity for much of the time. Later stage work was also inconsistent and generally below par.

By 1976, he was a shadow of his former self and on August 29 that year he suffered an epileptic fit and died in his sleep of respiratory failure at his Oakland, California, home. It was two years since the passing of his wife, Mary Lee "Mama" Davis, who was 20 years his junior but had written many of his most popular songs and given him nine children.

A stunningly individual performer, Jimmy had, none the less, been a major influence not only on white musicians but on a wide range of black performers and it is tribute to the breadth of his appeal that one of the finest covers of one of his songs was the insistently bluesy mid-tempo version of 'You Got Me Running' cut by rock 'n' roll icon Little Richard.

BESSIE SMITH

Empress of the Blues

Singer
Born: April 15, 1894, Chatanooga, Tennessee, USA
Died: September 26, 1937, Clarksdale, Mississippi, USA

THERE WERE SEVERAL CLAIMANTS TO THE TITLE "QUEEN OF THE BLUES"—VICTORIA SPIVEY, MAMIE SMITH, IDA COX, CLARA SMITH AND MA RAINEY AMONG THEM. BUT BESSIE SMITH WAS MORE THAN ALL THAT—SHE WAS THE UNDISPUTED "EMPRESS OF THE BLUES".

Her life story—from the early death of her parents and her singing on the streets for pennies, through the hard times and the good times to mass popular recognition and her tragic death—was the stuff of legends while her music retains its immense power and depth of emotion to this day, transcending the limitations of primitive recording techniques. Bessie was, without doubt, the greatest black recording artist of her era—in terms of both artistry and commercial success—her majestic big voice and superb phrasing and diction straddling the realms of blues, jazz and popular singing.

She was born in the renowned railroad town of Chatanooga, Tennessee, on April 15, 1894, one of the seven children of William and Laura Smith, and orphaned at the age of 8. As a teenager, Bessie built a reputation locally and by 1912 was to be found on the same bill as Ma Rainey for a show at the Ivory Theatre in her home town before setting off to tour as a chorus girl in Irvin C Miller's tent show.

In 1915, Bessie again worked with Ma Rainey, in Fat Chappelle's Rabbit Foot Minstrels Show, touring the South, and three years later starred as a singer, dancer and male impersonator in her own Liberty Belles Revue at the 91 Theatre in Atlanta. By the early Twenties she had gravitated to the East Coast, working prolifically in Philadelphia and Jersey City before being signed by Columbia Records.

In June 1923, Bessie embarked on a major tour. Her first recordings had just been released, to an overwhelming response—'Down Hearted Blues' alone selling more than 800,000 copies.

Her career was flying high, her name on the billboards pulling standing-room-only audiences to major theatres throughout the land as she headlined her own revues under such titles as *The Harlem Frolics Show*, *The Yellow Girls Revue*, and *Steamboat Days*. She appeared in the RCA Phototone two-reel film short *St Louis Blues* and became a massively popular draw at Harlem's renowned Apollo Theatre.

The biggest-selling black artist of her day, Bessie Smith was truly the Empress of the Blues.

Although primarily known for her blues recordings, Bessie was equally at home with jazz, vaudeville and Tin Pan Alley material and even recorded duets with Clara Smith, featuring the recently formed Fletcher Henderson Big Band, with the then 19-year old Coleman Hawkins on tenor saxophone.

By the end of 1929, Bessie's voice had grown somewhat rougher edged and she was also suffering the cumulative effects of vaudeville theatre—the classic blues singer's most important medium—being killed by radio, record sales being killed by the financial disaster of the Depression, and a serious gin-drinking problem.

On May 8 that year she had recorded three blatantly pornographic tunes, written by Andy Razaf, Fats Waller's lyricist. A week later, she recorded 'Nobody Knows You When You're Down And Out', truly a theme for those troubled times and surely her finest, most poignant record.

From August through to October 1929 Bessie recorded ten majestic sides with her favourite pianist, James P. Johnson—memorable collaborations between two great artists at the peak of their powers. Within two weeks of those sessions, the stock market had crashed.

Where her mid-Twenties records had regularly sold 20,000 or 30,000 copies, by 1930 'Keep It To Yourself' could only manage 4,150 and when her last Columbia release, 'Shipwreck Blues', was issued in July 1932 sales dropped to a mere 400.

Stage work kept her career alive though, and by 1937 Bessie was drawing rave reviews for her showcase slot on John Hammond's *From Spirituals To Swing* show at Carnegie Hall. Sadly, though, while touring Southern theatres with the Broadway Rastus Revue she was involved in a bad car accident at Coahoma, Mississippi. Refused admission at a whites-only hospital, she was rushed to the Afro-American Hospital in Clarksdale, where her arm had to be amputated. The delay, shock and loss of blood proved too much and on September 26, 1937, she died.

T-BONE WALKER

Swinging the Blues

Singer/Songwriter/Guitarist/Pianist
Born: May 28, 1910, Linden, Texas, USA
Died: March 16, 1975, Los Angeles, USA

*N*O WONDER THEY CALLED HIM "THE DADDY OF THE BLUES"—
AARON THIBEAUX "T-BONE" WALKER WAS THE MAN WHO FIRST
TOOK THE MUSIC ELECTRIC IN A BIG WAY AND HAS BEEN CITED AS THE
MAJOR INFLUENCE ON SUCH ARTISTS AS B. B. KING, BUDDY GUY,
OTIS RUSH, JOHNNY "GUITAR" WATSON, CHUCK BERRY, MIKE
BLOOMFIELD AND DUANE ALLMAN.

Nobody could swing like this man—a talent honed from his years playing the pre-Second World War vaudeville circuits, where the frontiers of the blues and jazz were totally blurred. T-Bone had accompanied such greats as Ida Cox, Ma Rainey and Bessie Smith, besides serving as the replacement for jazz guitar pioneer Charlie Christian in the Lawson Brooks Orchestra and working for a time with Cab Calloway, who fired him for arriving late at a gig.

He was born in Linden, Texas, on May 28, 1910. His grandmother was a Cherokee Indian, his father, Rance Walker, and mother, Movelia Jimerson, were singers. When he was 2 years old, T-Bone's parents separated and he was sent to live with his grandfather, who owned a sawmill in the Dallas area. His unusual nickname was said to be a corruption of the Creole phrase "T'beau", meaning "Pretty One"—though a more prosaic and probable explanation is that it derives from his middle name of Thibeaux.

T-Bone's mother, his stepfather, Marco Washington, and his cousin, K. C. Smith, worked in a local string band and they taught the youngster to play the banjo.

Citing Scrapper Blackwell and Blind Lemon Jefferson as major influences, T-Bone gained early experience by leading Jefferson round the streets of Dallas, playing on street corners for nickels and dimes, before, at the age of 14, joining Dr Breeding's Big B Tonic Medicine Show and touring throughout Texas.

By the early Thirties, T-Bone had gathered a wealth of varied experience and had cut his first records—for the Black & White label. In 1935 he caught the train to Los Angeles and found work at the Little Harlem Club and other venues before a regular job with Les Hite's Cotton Club Orchestra took him across the USA to New York where he recorded 'T-Bone Blues' for Varsity. Returning to LA, T-Bone formed a small combo with pianist Freddie Slack and they made one record for Capitol before T-Bone moved to Chicago to work for Marl Young of the Rhumboogie Club and label. Independent once more, T-Bone found plenty of work between 1942 and 1945 playing at US Army bases and concert venues across the States as well as recording and playing dates with many of the top bands of the time, led by such luminaries as Lucky Millender, Jack McVea and Jay McShann.

Black & White continued to record him prolifically until selling the contract and all the old masters to Capitol in the late 1940s. Capitol gave him the star treatment and when that deal ran out there followed a fruitful five-year stint with Imperial Records, during which time many of T-Bone's best discs were cut.

Then an ulcerated stomach put him in hospital. The removal of two-thirds of his stomach meant that T-Bone had to adopt a very strict diet and could only work intermittently during a five-year recovery period.

By 1962, the first European blues boom was in

Texan giant T-Bone Walker pioneered electric blues.

full flight and T-Bone crossed the Atlantic as a member of the first American Folk Blues Festival roster, returning a number of times over the following decade, either as a solo or as part of package tours.

His career continued through to 1974 when illness caused his retirement. On March 16, 1975, T-Bone died of bronchial pneumonia in Vernon Convalescent Hospital, LA.

On his sleeve-note for a fine 1968 album recorded in Paris, Hot Club de France vice-president Jacques Morgantini summed up T-Bone's remarkable influence: "Anyone who, after 1940, wanted to play the blues on the electric guitar borrowed from T-Bone, either from his marvellous sound or from his melodic style. Nobody knew better than he how to make his instrument 'talk'.

"His timing was astonishing, each note, each sound, settled, enhanced in perfectly balanced, definitely structured phrases.

"He was also a brilliant singer, with an entrancing...voice and a style less...earthy than Big Bill, John Lee Hooker or Muddy Waters."

MUDDY WATERS

Father of the Electric Blues

Singer/Songwriter/Guitarist
Born: April 4, 1915, Rolling Fork, Mississippi, USA
Died: May 1983, Chicago, USA

M UDDY WATERS NOT ONLY MADE GREAT MUSIC IN HIS OWN RIGHT—HE PROVIDED THE CATALYST THAT MADE THE CHICAGO BLUES SCENE ARGUABLY THE MOST VIBRANT MUSIC CENTRE IN THE WORLD DURING ITS HEY-DAY FROM THE LATE FORTIES THROUGH TO THE EARLY SEVENTIES.

Not only did Muddy both inspire and encourage countless young musicians—not least among them being Buddy Guy and the young Rolling Stones—but his band served as a spawning ground for a veritable roll-call of talent.

Jimmy Rogers, Little Walter, Freddie Below, Junior Wells, Big Walter Horton, James Cotton, Pat Hare, Matt Murphy, Luther Tucker, Sam Lawhorn, Luther Johnson and his own reputed half-brother Otis Spann were just a few of the many remarkable players who were proud to play alongside the master and, in later times, a whole coterie of young white rock stars, both American and British, played tribute by joining him on his albums.

In the tradition of the great Delta bluesmen, Muddy—who was born McKinley Morganfield in rural Rolling Fork, Mississippi, on April 4, 1915—learned his craft from his elders, in his case directly from Son House, the same man who had earlier groomed the legendary Robert Johnson. It was House who taught Muddy to play guitar bottleneck style.

His father raised hogs and chickens and Muddy earned his lifelong nickname from his sisters for rolling around in the creek.

He taught himself harmonica and guitar and worked at local parties and picnics through the Thirties. When Alan Lomax brought the Library of Congress field recording team to Stovall's Plantation in the summer of 1941, Muddy was still playing acoustically in the intense, brooding style of Son House and Robert Johnson. Little did they realize that they were recording for posterity the emergent talent of a young man who would go on to be a giant of the electric blues.

Within a year or so, Muddy had left the flat, low-lying Delta country for big city Chicago, where he discovered the value of using a cheap amplifier to boost up his music when playing for hand-outs on the crowded Maxwell Street market.

Gradually, Muddy learned his way round the local club scene, sitting in with such artists as John Lee

"Sonny Boy" Williamson, Tampa Red, Doc Clayton, his cousin Eddie Boyd and others and eventually forming his own seminal trio with fellow guitarist Jimmy Rogers and harmonica player Little Walter Jacobs. He soon enlarged the hard-rocking outfit to incorporate Sunnyland Slim, Leroy Foster, Johnny Jones and Otis Spann.

By 1947, Muddy was already cutting records for the newly formed Aristocrat label, which soon after changed its name to Chess—his home for the next 25 years. Initial releases featured just his guitar and Big Crawford's bass but he soon filled the sound out.

By the early Fifties, Muddy and his band were really steaming. The hits flowed, with such classics as 'Hoochie Coochie Man', 'Got My Mojo Working', 'Tiger In Your Tank', 'I Got My Brand On You' and 'I'm A Man'.

Between 1950 and 1958 Muddy enjoyed 12 major US R&B chart hits and when black audiences started turning their backs on the old blues sound, in favour of the more modern soul music, he was ready to capture new audiences among the white rock fans, even offering them a remarkable rearview mirror glimpse of his roots via the brooding *Muddy Waters—The Folk Singer* acoustic set.

After he stole the show at the 1960 Newport Jazz Festival, Waters became increasingly international in his outlook. Eventually, for purists, he went too far, recording in the psychedelic era the weird progressive rock hybrid albums *Electric Mud* and *Father And Sons* and a London studio set using British rock musicians.

With the demise of Chess as a creative label in the early Seventies, Muddy found a new home on the Blue Sky label owned by Johnny Winter.

In 1976, Muddy was one of the first blues musicians to visit Eastern Europe, playing the Jazz Jamboree show in Warsaw, and through the next couple of years toured intensively in Europe and the US.

Muddy died in May 1983. His legend lives on and has come to epitomize the ensemble style of playing which characterizes the classic Chicago urban blues.

Father-figure of Chicago's blues scene—Muddy Waters.

'DUST MY BROOM'

F OR MANY, IT WAS ROBERT JOHNSON WHO FIRST DEFIN-ED THE SHAPE OF MODERN BLUES, THOUGH HE NEVER LIVED LONG enough to profit from the mass migration to Chicago which saw the music go big, brash and electric, in the process carrying many of his contemporaries to international adulation and, despite the notorious rip-offs that blighted the record industry, not inconsiderable fortune.

Johnson himself had borrowed elements of his innovative style from others, notably Son House, the true pioneer of bottleneck guitar playing, in which a piece of glass or metal is slipped over the finger and run along the string to produce an eerie, whining effect.

Many of Johnson's songs have transcended the limitations of the blues and entered the rock genre. He was truly, as writer Sam Charters observed: "The root source for a whole generation of blues and rock 'n' roll musicians." Yet, ironically, one of his very finest compositions, originally titled 'I Believe I'll Dust My Broom', exerted its magic not through his own crackly 78 rpm recording of the Thirties but from the strident Fifties version laid down for Trumpet Records in Jackson, Mississippi, by one Elmore James.

What's more, Elmore James and his cousin Homesick James took that riff from 'Dust My Broom' and turned it into the cornerstone of a dozen more songs, from 'Dust My Blues' through to the rhythm track behind Big Joe Turner's 'TV Mama'.

It also provided the life blood for dozens of young white British blues bands—in smoky blues clubs and in the recording studio alike—as the great Sixties R&B explosion gathered momentum.

John Mayall's Bluesbreakers, with Eric Clapton on lead guitar, Chicken Shack, and the emergent Fleetwood Mac, featuring the talents of Peter Green and Jeremy Taylor, each in turn churned out their own faithful renditions of Elmore James's exciting sound, making 'Dust My Broom' the clarion call for a generation.

'BIG BOSS MAN'

W HILE THEIR SOUL-SLANTED CONTEMPORARIES WERE BELTING OUT ENDLESS REPETITIONS OF WILSON PICKETT'S 'IN THE Midnight Hour', hundreds of British and European products of the mid-Sixties R&B explosion—from purists like the Bob Brunning Sunflower Blues Band through to commercially orientated acts like the Animals—turned their attention to the Jimmy Reed songbook.

Of all the great American influences, Reed offered the attraction of almost overwhelming simplicity—his songs being easy for even the most limited of musicians to tackle without any great difficulty.

The Rolling Stones unashamedly cribbed Reed's 'Shame, Shame, Shame', gave it new lyrics and, under the guise of 'Little By Little' recorded one of their earliest hits, while even veteran rock 'n' roller Little Richard couldn't resist such easy pickings, cutting a superb version of 'You Got Me Running'

which helped reinstate his career after one of his periodic escapes into the world of hot gospel music and sermonizing.

That brilliant black American comedian of the Seventies, Franklyn Ajaye, once commented of James Brown: "What a genius! 'Good God There Is My Woman', 'There Is My Woman Good God'—two hits!!"—and cynics could make a similar comment about Reed, so many of whose songs had the same basic loping tempo, rhythm and backbeat, not to say melody.

But even they could surely not deny the hypnotic power of Reed's music—quintessential 12-bar magic rooted in the Mississippi Delta, honed in vibrant big-city Chicago and purveyed to the world.

'Peepin' And Hidin'', 'You Got Me Dizzy', 'Hush Your Mouth', 'Bright Lights, Big City', and many more all worked the same familiar mode—but perhaps the most influential of all was 'Big Boss Man', not only a hit for Reed, but a song since covered by so many other acts, black and white alike.

'STORMY MONDAY'

J -BONE WALKER'S 'STORMY MONDAY BLUES' IS IN MANY WAYS THE ARCHETYPAL BLUES STANDARD—COVERED BY SO MANY other artists, in so very many different ways.

It is such a versatile song, indeed, that rather than faithfully following T-Bone's original—a hit way back in the early Fifties—each artist was able to add his or her own indelible stamp to the tune.

A consummate showman who duck-walked across major theatre stages when Chuck Berry was still an unknown and played guitar with his teeth and behind his neck years before Jimi Hendrix used the gimmicks to become the darling of international rock audiences, Walker himself was a product of the Texas/California school of bluesmen.

His electric guitar playing style was as much influenced by the jazz of Charlie Christian and Django Reinhardt as it was by the work of the great Delta and Chicago blues players. Soul singer Lou Rawls similarly chose a heavy jazz flavour for his superlative version of 'Stormy Monday Blues', cut live for Capitol at a Chicago night club and using jazz stars Les McCann and Leroy Vinegar as his backing musicians.

The enormously talented Rawls not only brought a whole new level of sophistication into the blues but also, with the lengthy spoken-over-music intro to 'Stormy Monday', provided an early example of the rap style of delivery which would later be taken up by James Brown and Isaac Hayes and then, in the late Eighties, create a whole new style of black music.

In contrast, Bobby "Blue" Bland, who for many years made the song a centrepiece of his dynamic stage show, chose a brass-laden big-band format fronted jointly by his own superb voice and the majestic guitar-playing of longtime collaborator Wayne Bennett, using "call and response" patterns which, while the ultimate in modern uptown blues, harked back to the worksongs and field calls of the slavery era.

'EVERY DAY I HAVE THE BLUES'

T HERE ARE THOSE WHO WOULD ARGUE THAT CERTAIN BLUES ARTISTS—NOTABLY JOSH WHITE, LEADBELLY, BIG "BILL" Broonzy and the Sonny Terry/ Brownie McGhee partnership— have, because of a natural flair for self-publicity, achieved international reputations which far exceed the true importance of their contribution to the development of the blues music idiom as a great American art form.

Another name that regularly features in this rather specious argument is that of Memphis Slim, or Peter Chatman, as he was born. Such pedants would point out that even the name which carried him to stardom was not really his own invention, the "Memphis Slim" tag having far earlier been employed by the classy barrelhouse pianist Cow Cow Davenport, who had been one of his early influences.

This big, hulking man, who had a penchant for staying at the Dorchester and living the high society life which was so far removed from the hard, cruel world of the Deep South in which the blues was born, was undoubtedly adept at playing the main chance to his advantage. It is wrong, however, to allow all this to overshadow the strength of his artistic creativity.

If for nothing else, he has earned his place in the pantheon of blues greats for writing 'Everyday I Have The Blues', a number which must surely rank as among the most played of all compositions in the idiom. Should one wish to run a book on the blues standards most likely to be included in any artist's on-stage repertoire then a fair chunk of the wise money would go on this particular anthem.

Not only is it a remarkably infectious tune guaranteed to stick in the mind, but the lyrics encapsulate all the reasons why a fair number of black American musicians still turn inexorably to the blues as their most potent form of expression.

'DRIFTIN' BLUES'

*D*ESPITE ITS WELL-DEFINED AND, SOME MIGHT ARGUE, RATHER CONSTRICTED GENERAL FORMAT, THE BLUES IS AN ASTONISHINGLY versatile musical idiom. Born of poverty, the blues gave powerful voice to the fears, the frustrations and the despair of the dispossessed but, in other moments, it could set spirits soaring high, get dancers hopping, and show that fun can survive even amid crushing misery.

While most songs are of the "I've got two feet in the gutter, ain't life a bitch?" variety, the blues sing of joy as well as of pain. Indeed, at times they can be almost stridently optimistic—as in Bobby "Blue" Bland's powerful 'Ain't Doin' Too Bad', for example.

Undoubtedly, though, as with all music forms, the blues are at their most potent when the story is of cheating love and yearning hearts. And when the love is totally forlorn, how easy it is to wallow in the waves of self-pity: "Well I'm drifting and I'm drifting/Like a ship out on the sea."

Few songs have ever possessed such melancholy or been so haunting. For writer/performer Charles Brown and the Aladdin label, to which he was affiliated, 'Driftin' Blues' spelt a 1946 million-seller and an honoured place in blues history.

An educated man, who held a bachelor of science degree in chemistry and maths and had been a schoolteacher, Brown was to be a major influence over such greats as Johnny Ace, Ray Charles, B. B. King, Amos Milburn and, most notably, Floyd Dixon.

'Driftin' Blues', for its part, was to give the redoubtable Chuck Berry one of his few chances to step across the threshold from rock 'n' roll into the blues. Berry's cover version was every bit as good as Brown's original, so too was the much later rendition laid down in New Orleans by Guitar Slim.

If the blues is supposed to be all about touching the emotions, then 'Driftin' Blues' must rate as a blues classic *par excellence*.

'HOOCHIE COOCHIE MAN'

*W*HILE THERE HAVE BEEN NUMEROUS WONDERFUL FEMALE EXPONENTS OF THE BLUES—FROM IDA COX, VICTORIA SPIVEY AND Bessie Smith through to Etta James and Koko Taylor—it has, unlike soul music, been largely a male domain. Many of its very best songs brag of masculine virility—from 'Little Red Rooster' and 'Backdoor Man', both recorded by Howlin' Wolf, to Bo Diddley's 'I'm A Man'.

That latter song was co-written and recorded with distinction by Muddy Waters. However, both Diddley and Waters—along with Howlin' Wolf and others on the Chess roster—also recorded many songs penned by Willie Dixon (the two Howlin' Wolf tracks mentioned above were his, for example).

An artist in his own right, Dixon was even more active as Chess Records' resident bass-player, songwriter and producer. Though he found his fame and fortune in Chicago, Dixon's roots were firmly planted in the rich alluvial soil of the Mississippi Delta. Folk themes from the Deep South ran through much of his material. He wrote of employing 'My John The Conquer Root', having fun at a 'Wang Dang Doodle', composed 'Hoo Doo Blues' and talked of being a 'Seventh Son' and a 'Hoochie Coochie Man'.

It was with his rousing version of 'Hoochie Coochie Man' and the equally strident and symbolic 'I Got My Mojo Working' that Muddy Waters tore up the 1960 Newport Jazz Festival, finally wresting urban electric blues from the confines of the black ghetto and winning it a worldwide audience.

Just as importantly, it was these memorable performances which persuaded dozens of white performers—with Alexis Korner and Cyril Davies in the vanguard and the emergent Rolling Stones following hard behind—to turn their backs on the acoustic country blues influenced skiffle music and become hard-rocking R&B outfits.

'RECONSIDER BABY'

*W*HILE TIN-PAN ALLEY TELLS OF ROMANCE AS WE WOULD LIKE IT TO BE—LOVE AT FIRST SIGHT, KISSES AND ROSES, HAPPY EVER AFTER— the blues has always told it like it really is, with no holds barred. Backdoor-creeping adultery, two-timing fornication, one-way affairs, broken hearts and vicious revenge are recurrent themes.

Lowell Fulsom's powerful plea to 'Reconsider Baby' was very much in this long tradition and surely ranks as one of the great classics of the genre. A classy songwriter, who also gave us such opuses as 'Every Second A Fool Is Born', 'It's Your Own Fault', 'Three O'Clock Blues and 'Tramp'—all of them big hits for other performers as well as for Fulsom himself—the Texan troubadour eschewed the somewhat sparse symbolism of Willie Dixon and others for songs which really laid it solidly on the line, spelling out

every ounce of misery and despair through their poetic lyrics.

In 'Reconsider Baby', the writer laid down a strong case for his departing lover to have a change of heart, to try to pick up and mend the broken pieces—despite all that had gone wrong. A heartfelt plea, tinged with desolation and self-pity, the song struck a highly personal chord with many of those who rushed out to buy the record and in the process put it high into the best-seller listings.

And those drowning their sorrows in sleazy bars, scruffy luncheonettes and cheap dance joints right across America dropped their nickels into countless juke boxes to hear the song one more time.

Other artists adopted the number as part of their own repertoire— most notably Bobby "Blue" Bland, whose own version was a real killer, one of the best recordings this prolific artist ever made.

Nearly 40 years on, 'Reconsider Baby' is a song which still sounds as universally relevant as it did on the day when it was written.

'THE THRILL IS GONE'

*U*NLIKE MOST BLUES CLASSICS, THERE HAVE NOT BEEN TOO MANY COVERS OF 'THE THRILL IS GONE'—AN EXCEPTION BEING the reading by Little Milton, but you would certainly expect him to have tackled the song. After all, Milton has spent so much of his long career shadowing B. B. King, both as a guitarist and a singer.

It isn't that the song is not notable—the reluctance of others to include it in their repertoire being more likely due to B.B.'s version not only having been so definitive but being very hard to emulate, given its innovative use of strings, a brave venture at the time of its recording in the late Sixties.

Not that B.B. had never flirted with full orchestral arrangements before—one of his early albums featured a massed string section and arrangements by Marty Paitch, a man better known for his work within the field of country and western music. The bluesman's bluesman has long been a proponent of the theory that the relationship between Nashville and the Delta is far closer than most would believe: "Despite segregation, many of the experiences and the influences were shared. To me, country music has always been the white man's blues. It evokes the same troubles and pleasures, taps the same emotional vein," B.B. once said.

Never one to be backwards in moving forwards, B.B. slotted the song on to *Completely Well*, a milestone album. It was recorded in a freewheeling jam-session-style New York celebration of his music.

Lifted as a single, the far more structured 'The Thrill Is Gone' transcended the restrictions of the R&B charts and became B.B.'s biggest hit up to that time—a massive pop smash in a number of markets both outside and inside the USA. Most importantly, it proved that the blues could be complex, sophisticated music which appeals to the intellect as well as to the stronger basic emotions.

'MERRY CHRISTMAS BABY'

*I*T WAS THE BLUES WHICH GAVE ELVIS PRESLEY HIS EARLY INSPIRATION AND HIS FIRST HIT, WITH A COVER VERSION OF ARTHUR "Big Boy" Crudup's 'It's Alright Mama'. Raised in blues-rich Tupelo, Mississippi, and later in Memphis, the major centre of black music recording in the South, "the King" periodically returned to the blues idiom as a source for good songs.

Tucked away in one of his more maudlin albums—a bland collection of white spirituals—is a track which not only rates as one of his very best recordings ever but as a truly classic blues outing judged in any company, let alone merely that of white interpreters of the form.

Counterpointed by James Burton's inspired guitar playing—the instrumental break being a pure masterpiece of blues creativity—Elvis's rich baritone rings every ounce of emotion from a song which, though intended to sell against such other seasonal favourites as 'Rudolph The Red Nosed Reindeer', 'Jingle Bells' and 'White Christmas', is a serious blues composition which can be listened to at any time of the year.

Nor was Elvis the only major artist to cover this song, which had first come to prominence when Charles Brown's original scorched up the American R&B charts in 1948 (Brown himself remade the song during a New Orleans session in 1956 and was rewarded with a second-time-around hit).

Chuck Berry, who also covered Brown's 'Driftin' Blues', brought his own inimitable styling to 'Merry Christmas Baby' and showed that, had he chosen to go in that direction, instead of into the more lucrative world of rock 'n' roll, he could have been one of the greatest bluesmen of them all.

And then there was James Brown—"Soul Brother Number One"—who reached right back to his gospel roots to wail and scream his way through the song.

'LITTLE RED ROOSTER'

$\mathcal{D}$ ESPITE WHAT PURISTS MIGHT ARGUE TO THE CONTRARY, THE BRITISH R&B BOOM, WHILE LARGELY DERIVATIVE, DID NOW AND then bring forth bursts of originality, even when the songs were cover versions of American blues hits.

The Cyril Davies All-Stars' storming instrumental outing 'Country Line Special' was a wholly original effort. Rod Stewart utilized an old John Lee "Sonny Boy" Williamson composition, 'Good Morning Little Schoolgirl', for one of his rare sorties into blues territory; his jaunty version of that oft-recorded item was very different from the others, but none the worse for that.

On very rare occasions, the British cover actually surpassed the American waxings from which the inspiration came. This was arguably the case for Them's version of 'Baby Please Don't Go' and also for the Rolling Stones' version of Howlin' Wolf's 'Little Red Rooster'. The Wolf's version of 'Rooster' was magnificent, of course, but for British fans his meisterwerk was 'Smokestack Lightnin''—a record which, for all its uncompromising rawness, made the UK Top 20.

As for the Stones, they slowed 'Rooster' down, giving it a moody, brooding quality which used Mick Jagger's albeit limited vocal talents to best effect while Brian Jones and Keith Richard contributed complementary guitar breaks of authentic earthiness. But if the Rolling Stones arguably capped Howlin' Wolf on this one, then soul singer Sam Cooke's version, recorded shortly before his tragic death in a shooting in 1964, was even better still.

Backed by Billy Preston on electric organ and Ray Freeman on piano, and produced by the redoubtable Hugo and Luigi, the father of soul swung the song and made it his very own property in a performance which straddled the soul, R&B and blues styles of the day—and still sounds remarkably fresh all these years later.

blues•classics

THE STORY OF THE BLUES HAS, THANKFULLY, ALREADY BEEN WELL DOCUMENTED ON CD, BUT THE TRUE ENTHUSIAST WILL STILL HAVE TO RESORT TO VINYL IF HIS COLLECTION IS TO BE TRULY COMPREHENSIVE. OF COURSE, EVERYONE WILL HAVE THEIR OWN IDEAS ON THE ESSENTIAL RELEASES AROUND WHICH A SELF-RESPECTING COLLECTION SHOULD BE BUILT. THIS IS OUR PERSONAL CHOICE. SOME OF THEM HAVE ALREADY, WE ARE HAPPY TO SAY, BEEN REISSUED ON CD—SOMETIMES WITH ADDITIONAL CUTS—BUT FOR OTHERS YOU WILL HAVE TO SEARCH THE SECONDHAND SHOPS AND AUCTION LISTS. YOU MAY FIND YOU WILL HAVE TO PAY A LOT OF MONEY FOR SOME OF THEM, SO COLLECTABLE HAVE THEY BECOME OVER THE YEARS.

THE SEARCH AND THE FINANCIAL INVESTMENT WILL BE WORTHWHILE FOR THESE 15 ALBUMS WOULD ON THEIR OWN CONSTITUTE A WELL-ROUNDED AND COVETABLE COLLECTION. MOST IMPORTANTLY, THOUGH, APART FROM THEIR INTRINSIC VALUE, THEY WILL PROVIDE MANY HOURS OF LISTENING PLEASURE.

THE BLUES ROL...
ATLANTIC, 1960

'BOOGIE CHILDREN' (BOY BLUE, WILLIE JONES AND JOE LEE); 'SHE LIVED HER LIFE TOO FAST' (FOREST CITY JOE); 'DROP DOWN MAMA' (MISSISSIPPI FRED MCDOWELL); 'SITTIN' ON TOP OF THE WORLD' (LONNIE & ED YOUNG, LONNIE YOUNG JR.); 'COOL WATER BLUES' (JOHN DUDLEY); 'SHE DON'T LOVE ME THAT WAY' (FOREST CITY JOE); 'STOP BREAKING DOWN' (FOREST CITY JOE); 'JOE LEE'S ROCK' (BOY BLUE, WILLIE JONES AND JOHN LEE); 'BULLYIN' WELL' (ROSALIE HILL); 'WHEN YOU GET HOME, WRITE ME A FEW LITTLE LINES' (MISSISSIPPI FRED MCDOWELL); 'RED CROSS STORE' (FOREST CITY JOE); ' FOREST CITY JUMP' (FOREST CITY JOE).

Part of Atlantic's memorable *Southern Folk Heritage* series, this set was the result of one of Alan Lomax's field trips to the South. It not only introduced the world to the acoustic roots music of Fred McDowell, which he had previously only played to friends and relatives, but showcased Forest City Joe, a fresh, raw talent who would, like McDowell, have gone on to greater things had he not been accidentally killed just months later.

FOLK FESTIVAL OF THE BLUES
CHESS, 1964

'WEE WEE BABY' (MUDDY WATERS, WILLIE DIXON AND BUDDY GUY); 'SITTING AND THINKING' (MUDDY WATERS); 'WORRIED BLUES' (BUDDY GUY); 'BRING IT ON HOME' (SONNY BOY WILLIAMSON); 'CLOUDS IN MY HEART' (MUDDY WATERS); 'MAY I HAVE A TALK WITH YOU' (HOWLIN' WOLF); 'GOT MY MOJO WORKING' (MUDDY WATERS); 'DON'T KNOW WHICH WAY TO GO' (BUDDY GUY); 'SHE'S 19 YEARS OLD' (MUDDY WATERS)

Frank Zappa once said: "Anyone who can remember the Sixties couldn't have been there", but what self-respecting blues aficionado could forget the remarkable American Folk Festival Of The Blues touring packages which brought the music's finest

The electrifying Buddy Guy was a Folk Blues Festival stalwart.

exponents across the Atlantic to stun European audiences with their powerful sounds? This particular aggregation was a vintage one—probably the best of them all—with Waters, Guy, Williamson and Wolf at the very peak of their form.

BOBBY "BLUE" BLAND

TWO STEPS FROM THE BLUES
VOCALION, 1960

'TWO STEPS FROM THE BLUES'; 'CRY, CRY, CRY'; 'I'M NOT ASHAMED'; 'DON'T CRY NO MORE'; 'LEAD ME ON'; 'I PITY THE FOOL'; 'I'VE GOT TO FORGET YOU'; 'LITTLE BOY BLUE'; 'ST JAMES' INFIRMARY'; 'I'LL TAKE CARE OF YOU'; 'I DON'T WANT NO WOMEN'; 'I'VE BEEN WRONG SO LONG'

For many years a rare and highly sought-after item, this classic set of sophisticated Memphis/Houston style urban blues is now fairly easy to find on CD, failing which Ace's issue *The Voice* (CDCHD 323) con-

Bobby Bland merged gospel roots with the blues as a forerunner of soul music.

tains most of these tracks and much more besides.

With its strong gospel influence, this superlative album spotlights the beginnings of soul music's marriage of spiritual fervour with secular lyrics. Framed by Joe Scott's potent arrangements, the musicianship of the brass-laden Bill Harvey Orchestra and Wayne Bennett's virtuoso guitar playing, Bobby alternately wails, snarls and warm-voicedly charms his way through a great selection of songs which make it easy to understand how he has logged total record sales in excess of 25 million copies.

RAY CHARLES

RAY CHARLES IN RHYTHM & BLUES GREATS
REALM, 1963

'I FOUND MY BABY THERE' (RAY CHARLES); 'GUITAR BLUES' (RAY CHARLES); 'I WONDER WHY' (LIGHTNIN' HOPKINS); 'BUCK DANCE BOOGIE' (LIGHTNIN' HOPKINS); 'JUNCO PARTNER' (JAMES WAYNE); 'PLEASE BABY, PLEASE' (JAMES WAYNE); 'GOIN' DOWN SLOW' (SONNY TERRY); 'MEAN OLD FRISCO' (BROWNIE MCGHEE); 'FEELING BLUE AND LOW' (ARBEE STIDHAM); 'I'M IN THE MOOD' (ARBEE STIDHAM); 'SHAKE A LEG' (SMOKEY HOGG); 'I LOVE YOU BABY' (SMOKEY HOGG)

One of the first—and best—blues compilation albums issued in the UK, this set was released by a subsidiary of Oriole, an independent label also notable for giving Tamla Motown its first UK successes but which was bought soon after to provide the foundation for the giant CBS setup.

Much of the material contained on this album was recorded quite informally in hotel suites and the back rooms of record stores. It is raw, pungent blues from a diversity of sources—being cut variously in Florida, Atlanta, Houston and other locations. Unusually for a compilation, there's not a duff track within hearing.

The mood is rough, raw and almost primitive—yet most of it is urban rather than country blues in form and content.

Justifiably tagged as "the Genius", Ray Charles performed black music in varied forms.

THE ROBERT CRAY BAND

BAD INFLUENCE
DEMON, 1984

'PHONE BOOTH'; 'BAD INFLUENCE'; 'THE GRINDER'; 'GOT TO MAKE A COMEBACK'; 'SO MANY WOMEN, SO LITTLE TIME'; 'WHERE DO I GO FROM HERE'; 'WAITING FOR THE TIDE TO TURN'; 'MARCH ON'; 'DON'T TOUCH ME'; 'NO BIG DEAL'

The emergence of Robert Cray at the spearhead of a new generation of black American blues stars confirmed that the music is not stuck forever in a time-warp but will continue to develop and prosper for many years to come.

Rather than the bad influence hinted at in this LP's title, Robert Cray has been nothing but a good influence, not only bringing a fresh new approach onto the scene but also helping to cultivate the renewed prosperity of John Lee Hooker and B. B. King's careers, thus providing the bridge between the vintage and the vanguard.

This was Cray's second album and breakthrough to stardom. Although he veered towards soul and rock, Cray is a bluesman for today.

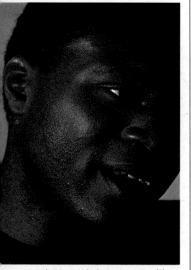

Robert Cray, spearheading a new generation of bluesmen.

LOWELL FULSOM

TRAMP
KENT, 1965

'TRAMP'; 'I'M SINKIN''; 'GET YOUR GAME UP TIGHT'; 'BACK DOOR KEY'; 'TWO WAY WISHING'; 'LONELY DAY'; 'BLACK NIGHTS'; 'YEAR OF 29'; 'NO HARD FEELINGS'; 'HUSTLERS GAME'; 'GOIN' HOME'; 'PICO'

Clean and sharp, Oklahoma-born Lowell Fulsom (spelt Fulson on many of his records) has been a mainstay of the West Coast blues scene for many years and helped propel his one-time sideman Ray Charles to stardom. With arrangements from the highly-rated Maxwell Davis, this seminal album served as a bridge between urban blues and the low-down gutbucket variety of deep soul music.

'Tramp' was lifted from this set to provide Otis Redding and Carla Thomas with a song which gave them a duet hit. The instrumental version, titled 'Pico', is also featured here, among other strong cuts.

JOHN LEE HOOKER

FREE BEER AND CHICKEN
ABC, 1974

'MAKE IT FUNKY'; 'FIVE LONG YEARS'; '713 BLUES'; '714 BLUES'; 'ONE BOURBON, ONE SCOTCH, ONE BEER'; 'HOMEWORK'; 'BLUEBIRD'; 'SITTIN' ON TOP OF THE WORLD'; 'COLLAGE'

Described on its sleeve as "a fortuitous concatenation of events"—whatever that may mean—this is a strange and rather mysterious album from a blues maestro who is fond of surprising his audiences with quirky time changes and peculiar harmonic patterns but never previously or since to quite this degree.

Rumour has it that a number of big-name rock artists were involved in the sessions—and certainly the distinctive smoky voice of Joe Cocker can be picked out—but the sleeve carries no personnel details. Whatever, it's a gem.

Hooker's output was often quirky —but never to this extent.

LIGHTNIN' HOPKINS

LIGHTNIN' HOPKINS SINGS THE BLUES
REALM, 1968

'HOME IN THE WOODS'; 'TAP DANCE BOOGIE'; 'WORRIED BLUES'; 'ONE KIND OF FAVOUR'; 'UNTRUE BLUES'; 'FAST LIFE WOMAN'; 'MY HEART TO WEEP'; ' I'LL NEVER FORGET THE DAY'; 'BROKEN HEARTED BLUES'; 'LIGHTNIN'S GONE AGAIN'; 'EUROPEAN BLUES'; 'LIGHTNIN'S BLUES'

A cousin of Texas Alexander and a protégé of Lonnie Johnson and Blind Lemon Jefferson, Sam "Lightnin'" Hopkins cut more than 400 sides in his lengthy career. By the time this album appeared, it was said that more than 50 LPs of his work had already been issued.

Recorded between 1950 and 1951, these particular tracks showcase Lightnin' at his raw and powerful best, unaccompanied save for his own guitar and those beer-bottle tops studded into the heels of his shoes—a gimmick used to magic effect on 'Tap Dance Boogie'.

ELMORE JAMES

DUST MY BROOM
TOPLINE, 1984

'COMING HOME'; 'DUST MY BROOM'; 'EVERYDAY I HAVE THE BLUES'; 'FINE LITTLE MAMA'; 'I DONE SOMEBODY WRONG'; 'IT HURTS ME TOO'; 'PICKIN' THE BLUES'; 'LOOK ON YONDER WALL'; 'MEAN MISTREATING MAMA'; 'ROLLING AND TUMBLING'; 'STANDING AT THE CROSSROADS'; 'THE SKY IS CRYING'

Over the years, there have been a number of compilations of Elmore James's finest work, issued via a variety of record companies. This was one of the best and, what's more, it appeared on a budget label. These are the songs which essentially defined the modern bottleneck style of guitar playing—providing the inspiration for a legion of enthusiastic young white imitators.

A giant in every sense: the electrifying B. B. King.

B. B. KING

COMPLETELY LIVE AND WELL
CHARLY R&B, 1986

'DON'T ANSWER THE DOOR'; 'JUST A LITTLE LOVE'; 'MY MOOD'; 'SWEET LITTLE ANGEL'; 'PLEASE ACCEPT MY LOVE'; 'I WANT YOU SO BAD'; 'FRIENDS'; 'GET OFF MY BACK WOMAN'; 'LET'S GET DOWN TO BUSINESS'; 'WHY I SING THE BLUES'; 'SO EXCITED'; 'NO GOOD'; 'YOU'RE LOSIN' ME'; 'WHAT HAPPENED'; 'CONFESSIN' THE BLUES'; 'KEY TO MY KINGDOM'; 'CRYING WON'T HELP YOU'; 'YOU'RE MEAN'; 'THE THRILL IS GONE'

A two-record amalgam of two mid-

Sixties sets—*Live And Well* and *Completely Well* produced in New York by Bill Szymczyck, this CD marks the watershed of B. B. King's progress from being master of the black ghetto to a major star on the international rock circuit.

There's a side recorded live with his own band and three studio sides cut with such redoubtable sidemen as drummer Herb Lovelle, keyboard player Paul Harris, bass-player Jerry Jemmott and white guitarist Hugh McCracken, who trades licks with the King in inspired fashion, the groove getting so intense on the lengthy 'Crying Won't Help You'/'You're Mean' medley that B.B. is left gasping: "What y'all tryin' to do?—Kill me?" at the end.

LITTLE MILTON

LITTLE MILTON PLAYS BIG BLUES
CHECKER, 1966

'FEEL SO BAD'; 'RECONSIDER BABY';
'STORMY MONDAY'; 'WOKE UP THIS MORNING';

Guitar virtuoso and potent singer: Little Milton.

'HARD LUCK BLUES'; 'PLEASE, PLEASE, PLEASE';
'SWEET SIXTEEN'; 'FEVER'; 'SNEAKIN' AROUND';
'DON'T DECEIVE ME'; 'HAVE MERCY BABY';
'PART TIME LOVE'

Often compared vocally to Bobby Bland and, as a guitarist, to B. B. King, Little Milton is, despite the similarities in style, a major artist in his own right.

This landmark album, though, found him playing tribute to not only Bobby and B.B. but to a host of other major blues and R&B names— including Lowell Fulsom, T-Bone Walker, Little Johnny Taylor, Chuck Willis, Little Willie John, Lightnin' Hopkins and James Brown—with powerhouse versions of some of their classic songs.

His reading of Hopkins' 'Feel So Bad' is a veritable masterpiece and the album as a whole convinced critics of Milton's blues credentials.

IKE TURNER

ROCKIN' BLUES
STATESIDE, 1986

'PRANCING'; 'THE THINGS I USED TO DO
(I DON'T DO NO MORE)'; 'THE GULLY'; 'THINK';
'YOU'RE STILL MY BABY'; 'KATANGA'; 'TACKS IN
MY SHOES'; 'RIGHT ON'; 'ROCKIN' BLUES';
'THAT'S ALRIGHT'; 'BROKEN HEARTED'; 'IF YOU
LOVE ME LIKE YOU SAY (YOU WOULDN'T TREAT
ME LIKE YOU DO)'; 'BOOTIE UP'; '(YOU CAN
HAVE) THE CITY'; 'NECKIN''; 'THESE DREAMS';
'SOPPIN' MOLASSES'

Before drug dependency messed up his marriage, his career and his life, Ike Turner played a key role in the evolution of both blues and soul music as a talent scout, songwriter, producer and performer.

Though they were usually tucked away on Ike And Tina Turner albums, Ike did now and again record numbers which showcased his own talents as guitarist, pianist and singer. This fascinating compilation traces these tracks down the years from 1962 to 1973.

T-BONE WALKER

T-BONE WALKER SINGS THE BLUES
LIBERTY, 1959

'STROLLIN' WITH BONES';
'YOU DON'T LOVE ME'; 'YOU DON'T
UNDERSTAND'; 'SAY! PRETTY BABY'; 'TELL ME
WHAT'S THE REASON'; 'BLUE MOOD'; 'THE SUN
WENT DOWN'; 'TRAVELIN' BLUES'; 'EVIL HEARTED
WOMAN'; 'COLD COLD FEELING'; 'I GOT THE
BLUES AGAIN'; 'BLUES IS A WOMAN'

The best of the superb material which T-Bone cut for Imperial after arriving out on the West Coast from Texas, the songs here have a remarkably intimate and haunting quality. Just listening to 'Cold Cold Feeling' sends shivers running down the back—it is rare indeed for music to be as truly emotive as this.

Someone once described an early Bob Dylan album as being "music to commit suicide to". The same could be said of this remarkably evocative selection from a true master.

MUDDY WATERS

MUDDY WATERS AT NEWPORT
PYE JAZZ, 1960

'I GOT MY BRAND ON YOU'; 'I'M YOUR
HOOCHIE COOCHIE MAN'; 'BABY PLEASE DON'T
GO'; 'SOON FORGOTTEN'; 'TIGER IN YOUR TANK';
'I FEEL SO GOOD'; 'GOT MY MOJO WORKING';
'GOT MY MOJO WORKING (PART TWO)';
'GOODBYE NEWPORT BLUES'

Recorded live at the Newport Jazz Festival during the long hot summer of 1960, this was the album which really opened up a mass international audience for the hard-hitting Chicago ghetto music of Muddy Waters and his confrères. On that memorable day, the hard-rocking band comprised James Cotton on harmonica, Otis Spann on piano, Tat Harris on guitar, Andrew Stevenson on bass and Francis Clay on drums.

Harmonica wizard James Cotton was grounded in the Muddy Waters band.

HOWLIN' WOLF

HOWLIN' WOLF
CHESS, 1963

'SHAKE FOR ME'; 'THE RED ROOSTER';
'YOU'LL BE MINE'; 'WHO'S BEEN TALKIN'?';
'WANG DANG DOODLE'; 'LITTLE BABY';
'SPOONFUL'; 'GOING DOWN SLOW'; 'DOWN IN
THE BOTTOM'; 'BACK DOOR MAN'; 'HOWLIN'
FOR MY BABY'; 'TELL ME'

This album was one of the most coveted of all imports to the UK at a time when those who aspired to being top faces or part of the UK "in crowd" had their LPs shipped direct from the US.

Featuring material recorded between 1959 and 1962, this was almost a "Best Of" the mighty Wolf—add 'Smokestack Lightnin'' and one or two other seminal songs and it would have been just that. The whole album contains mighty music, and Howlin' Wolf's version of St Louis Jimmy's 'Going Down Slow' is staggeringly potent. A must for any collection.

CDlistings

There is a wealth of blues material now available on CD, though—with much of it being on specialist or imported labels—some items can take a lot of tracking down. While record companies have not been tardy in tapping into the rich vein of blues classics, some obscure artists are, as yet, poorly represented.

The following is a far from exhaustive listing of what is currently on catalogue, each entry chosen as being representative of the best of the particular artist's work. Included is a selection of the best various artist compilations; such items make a good starting point in building up a meaningful collection.

The artists are listed alphabetically, followed by their albums, also in alphabetical order. Each entry contains the name of the album and the year of CD release, followed by the record labels and catalogue numbers under which the albums have been released in CD format. Some companies only release blues issues in a single territory (usually the US or the UK) but make them readily available on import in the other major record markets. Also included are a number of deletions which are worth tracking down in the cut-out bins or second-hand record shops.

JOHNNY ACE
Memorial Album
For Johnny Ace *1988*
US: MCA 31183

JOHNNY ADAMS
Reconsider Me *1987*
UK: CHARLY CDCHARLY 89
Room With A View
Of The Blues *1991*
UK: DEMON FIENDCD 111
US: ROUNDER CD2059

LUTHER ALLISON
Life Is A Bitch *1988*
UK: EMI ENCORE ENC131C
Rich Man *1989*
UK: CHARLY R&B
CDCHARLY 201

MOSE ALLISON
Sings And Plays *1991*
UK: PRESTIGE CDJZD 007

ALBERT AMMONS AND THE RHYTHM KINGS
Boogie Woogie And
The Blues *1987*
UK: COMMODORE
CLASS 824 297 (DELETED 1991)

LAVERN BAKER
No CDs CURRENTLY AVAILABLE

CAREY BELL
Mellow Down And
Easy *1992*
US: BLIND PIG 4291

SCRAPPER BLACKWELL
Virtuoso Guitar *1991*
US: YAZOO YAZCFD 1019

BOBBY BLAND
Best Of Bobby
Bland *1988*
US: MCA 31219
The Voice *1991*
UK: ACE CDCHD 323
First Class Blues
1988
UK: MALACO MALCD 5000
US: MALACO MALCD 5000
Two Steps From The
Blues *1990*
UK: MCA MCACD 4160
US: MCA MCACD 27036

MIKE BLOOMFIELD
American Hero *1988*
UK: THUNDERBOLT CDTB 1009
US: MAGNUM 1009
Between A Hard
Place And The
Ground *1990*
UK: THUNDERBOLT CDTB 076
US: MAGNUM 76
Juke Boy Bonner
1960–67 *1991*
UK: FLYRIGHT FLY CD38

TINY BRADSHAW
Breaking Up The
House *1985*
UK: CHARLY CDCHARLY 43

LONNIE BROOKS
Bayou Lightning
1988
UK: SONET SNTCD 798
US: ALLIGATOR ALCD 4714
Satisfaction
Guaranteed *1991*
UK: ALLIGATOR ALCD 4799
US: ALLIGATOR ALCD 4799

Wound Up Tight
1990
UK: ALLIGATOR SNTCD 974
US: ALLIGATOR ALCD 4751

BIG BILL BROONZY
Good Time Tonight
1990
UK: CBS 4672472
House Rent Stomp
1991
UK: BLUES ENCORE CD 52007
Remembering Big
Bill Broonzy *1992*
UK: BEAT GOES ON
BGOCD 91

CHARLES BROWN
All My Life
1991
UK: BULLSEYE BLUES
NETCD 9501
Driftin' Blues *1992*
UK: CAPITOL CZ 503
US: EMI USA E21Y-97989
Hard Times And
Cool Blues *1990*
UK: SEQUEL NEXCD 133

**CLARENCE
"GATEMOUTH"
BROWN**
No Looking Back
1992
UK: ALLIGATOR ALCD 4804
US:ALLIGATOR ALCD 4804
Real Life *1988*
US: ROUNDER CD 2054
San Antonio
Ballbuster
1992
UK: CHARLY CD BM6

NAPPY BROWN
I Done Gone Over
1990
SWEDEN: MR R&B RBD 205
Tore Up 1991
UK: ALLIGATOR ALCD 4792

ROY BROWN
Laughing But
Crying 1991
SWEDEN: ROUTE 88 RBD2

RUTH BROWN
The Hits 1990
UK: OFFICIAL OFF 86053

WILD CHILD BUTLER
Devil Made Me
Do It 1991
UK: BLUE HORIZON
CDBLUM 014 (DELETED)

PAUL BUTTERFIELD
East West
1989
UK: WEA 960751-2
US: ELEKTRA 7315-2
Paul Butterfield
Blues Band
1989
UK: WEA 960647-2
US: ELEKTRA 7294-2

CAB CALLOWAY
Cab Calloway Story
1989
UK: DEJA VU DVRECD 22
(DELETED 1992)
Most Important
Recordings
1991
UK: OFFICIAL OFF 830412

CANNED HEAT
The Big Heat 1992
UK: EMI BOX SET CANNED
7802752
Boogie With
Canned Heat 1986
UK: SEE FOR MILES SEECD 62

**GUS CANNON'S JUG
STOMPERS**
Complete 1991
UK: YAZOO YAZCD 1082
US: YAZOO YAZ 1082

LEROY CARR
Blues Before Sunrise
1990
UK: CBS 4654632

Naptown Blues 1991
UK: ALDABRA ALB1011CD

CLARENCE CARTER
Touch Of Blues 1989
UK: ICHIBAN CDICH 1032
US: ICHIBAN CDICH 1032

RAY CHARLES
Blues Is My Middle
Name 1989
UK: OBJECT ENTERPRISES
ONN 37 (DELETED 1991)
The Classic Years
1991
UK: ESSENTIAL ESBCD 144
The Genius 1988
UK: EXEL XELCD 106
The Right Time 1987
UK: ATLANTIC 241 119-2

CLIFTON CHENIER
Bon Ton Roulet 1992

UK: ARHOOLIE ARH 345
US: ARHOOLIE ARH 345
King Of Zydeco
1991
UK: ACE CDCH 234
Zydeco Blues And
Boogie 1992
UK: ACE CDCHD 389
US: ARHOOLIE 301

CHICKEN SHACK
Chicken Shack
Collection 1990
UK: CASTLE COLLECTOR
CCSCD179

ERIC CLAPTON
Back Trackin' 1990
UK: RSO 8219372
Early Collection
1987 (deleted 1992)
UK: CASTLE CCSCD 162

PEE WEE CLAYTON
Telephone Is
Ringing 1992
UK: PRESTIGE CDSGP008

EDDIE CLEARWATER
Blues Hangout 1991
UK: BLACK & BLUE BLE 59732
Help Yourself 1992
US: BLIND PIG 4792

GARY B. B. COLEMAN
Best Of Gary B. B.
Coleman 1990
UK: ICHIBAN ICH 1065 CD
US: ICHIBAN ICH 1065 CD
Romance Without
Finance Is A
Nuisance 1991

UK: ICHIBAN ICH 1107 CD
US: ICHIBAN ICH 1107 CD

ALBERT COLLINS
Cold Snap 1992
UK: ALLIGATOR ALCD 4752
US: ALLIGATOR ALCD 4752
Complete Imperial
Recordings 1991
UK: IMPERIAL CDS 7967412
Don't Lose Your
Cool 1990
UK: ALLIGATOR ALCD 4730
US: ALLIGATOR ALCD 4730
Ice Pickin' 1988
UK: ALLIGATOR ALCD 4713
US: ALLIGATOR ALCD 4713

JOHNNY COPELAND
Texas Twister 1988
US: ROUNDER CD 11504
When The Rain
Starts Fallin' 1988
UK: ROUNDER CD 11515
US: ROUNDER CD 11515

JAMES COTTON
High Compression
1986
UK: SONET SNTD 928
US: ALLIGATOR ALCD 4737
Live From Chicago
1990
UK: ALLIGATOR ALCD 4746
US: ALLIGATOR ALCD 4746
Mighty Long Time
1991
UK: ANTONES ANTCD 15
US: ANTONES 15

IDA COX
I Can't Quit My

Man 1991
UK: AFFINITY CDAFS 1015

ROBERT CRAY
Bad Influence 1986
UK: MERCURY 830245-2
US: HIGHBONE 8001
False Accusations
1986
UK: DEMON FIEND CD 43
US: HIGHBONE 8005
Strong Persuader
1986
UK: MERCURY 830.568-2
US: POLYGRAM 83056-2
Who's Been Talkin'
1988
UK: CHARLY CDCLM 101

ARTHUR CRUDUP
Roebuck Man 1992
UK: SEQUEL NEXCD 210
That's All Right
Mama 1992
UK: BLUEBIRD ND 90653
US: RCA 61043-2

**REVD BLIND GARY
DAVIS**
From Blues To
Gospel 1992
US: BIOGRAPH BCD 124
Pure Religion And
Bad Company
1992
UK: ROUNDER FS 40035
US: FOLKWAYS 40038

JIMMY DAWKINS
Feel The Blues
1988
UK: JSP CD 206

133

Kant Sheck Dees
Blues *1991*
UK: BLUE STING 024
US: EARWIG 4920

SUGAR PIE DESANTO
Use What You Got
1991
UK: CHARLY CDRED 33

WILLIE DIXON
Hidden Charms *1991*
UK: SILVERTONE LRECD 515
US: CAPITOL C21Y 90595
Willie Dixon *1990*
UK: MCA BOXED SET CHD
216500
US: MCA BOXED SET CHD
216500

**CHAMPION JACK
DUPREE**
Blues For Everybody
1990
UK: CHARLY CDCHARLY 243
From New Orleans
To Chicago *1988*
UK: DECCA 820568-2
US: POLYGRAM 820569-2
For Ever And Ever
1990
UK: BULLSEYE 9512
US: BULLSEYE NETCD 9512

SNOOKS EAGLIN
Baby You Can Get
Your Gun *1992*
UK: DEMON FIENDCD 96
Out Of Nowhere
1990
UK: DEMON FIENDCD 146
US: BLACK TOP 1046

RONNIE EARL
Deep Blues *1988*
US: BLACK TOP CD 1033
Peace Of Mind *1990*
UK: DEMON FIENDCD 169

HONEYBOY EDWARDS
Delta Bluesman *1992*
UK: INDIGO IGOCD 2003

SLEEPY JOHN ESTES
Sleepy John Estes
(1929–37) *1991*
UK: DOCUMENT DOCD 5015
Sleepy John Estes
(1937–41) *1991*
UK: DOCUMENT DOCD 5016
I Ain't Gonna Sleep
No More *1991*
UK:YAZOO YACD 2004
US: YAZOO YA 2004

FLEETWOOD MAC
Original Fleetwood
Mac *1991*
UK: ESSENTIAL ESSCD 026
The Blues Collection
(Live) *1989*
UK: CASTLE COLLECTOR
CCSCD 216
The Blues Years
1991
UK: ESSENTIAL BOX SET
ESBCD 138

BLIND BOY FULLER
1935–1940
1991
UK: TRAVELLIN' MAN TMCD 01
East Coast Piedmont
Blues *1991*
UK: COLUMBIA 4679232

JESSE FULLER
San Francisco Bay
Blues *1991*
US: OR BLUES COJBCD 537-2

JOHNNY FULLER
Fuller's Blues *1988*
NETHERLANDS: DIVING DUCK
DDCD 4311

LOWELL FULSOM
It's A Good Day
1988
US: ROUNDER CD 2088
Reconsider Baby
1989
UK: CHARLY CDRED 15
Hung Down Head
1991
UK: CHESS CHD 9325
US: CHESS 9325
Tramp And Soul
1991
UK: ACE CDCHD 339

SLIM GAILLARD
Legendary McVouty
1990
UK: HEP JAZZ HEPCD 6

CECIL GANT
Cecil Gant *1990*
UK: KRAZY KAT KKCD 03

DAVEY GRAHAM
Folk Blues And All
Points In Between
1990
UK: SEE FOR MILES SEECD 48

OTIS GRAND
He Knows The

Blues *1992*
UK: SEQUEL NEX CD 219

AL GREEN
Green Is Blues/
Gets Next To You
1990
UK: HI HIUKCD 106

**GUITAR JUNIOR
(LONNIE BROOKS)**
The Crawl *1992*
UK: CHARLY CD BM1

GUITAR SLIM
Story Of My Life
1992
UK: SKY RANCH SR 652311
US: ORLEANS 4188
Things That I Used
To Do *1991*
UK: ACE CDCHD 318

BUDDY GUY
Complete Chess
Studio Recordings
1992
UK: MCA CHD2 9337
US: MCA CHD2 9337
Damn Right I've
Got The Blues *1991*
UK: SILVERTONE ORECD 516
US: NOVUS 14622
First Time I Met
The Blues *1992*
UK: BLUES ENCORE CD 52015

JOHN HAMMOND
Best Of John
Hammond *1989*
UK: START YNP 7314
Got Love If You

Want It *1992*
UK: POINT BLANK YPBCD 7
US: VIRGIN V21S 86285
Nobody But You
1992
UK: DEMON FIENDCD 107
US: FLYING FISH FFCD 502

SLIM HARPO
I'm A King Bee *1989*
UK: FLYRIGHT FLYCD 05
Te-Ni-Nee-Ni-Nu
(The Best Of Slim
Harpo) *1991*
GERMANY: REPERTOIRE REP
4206-WZ

PEPPERMINT HARRIS
Sittin' In With
Peppermint Harris
1992
UK: MAINSTREAM MCD 907

WYNONIE HARRIS
Battle Of The Blues
(with Roy Brown)
1988
UK: CHARLY CD CHARLY 37
Good Rocking
Tonight *1991*
UK: CHARLY CDCHARLY 244
Mr Blues Is Coming
To Town *1991*
UK: MR R&B RBD3

Z. Z. HILL
Best Of Z. Z. Hill
1987
UK: MALACO MALCD 342

SMOKEY HOGG
Angels In Harlem

1992
UK: Ace CDHCD 419
US: Specialty 7020
**Sittin' In With
Smokey Hogg** *1992*
UK: Mainstream MDCD 906

BILLIE HOLIDAY
**Best Of Billie
Holiday** *1991*
UK: CBS 4670292
Billie's Blues *1988*
UK: Blue Note BNZ 110
Legacy 1933–58 *1991*
UK: Columbia Box set
4690492
US: Sony 47724

EARL HOOKER
**Two Bugs And A
Roach** *1992*
US: Arhoolie ARH 324

JOHN LEE HOOKER
**Best Of John Lee
Hooker** *1991*
UK: Music Club MCCD 020
**Free Beer And
Chicken** *1991*
UK: Beat Goes On
BGOCD 123
The Healer *1989*
UK: Silvertone ORECD 508
US: Chameleon 748082
**John Lee Hooker
Story** *1989*
UK: Deja Vu DVRECD 19

LIGHTNIN' HOPKINS
**Complete Prestige
And Bluesville
Recordings** *1991*

UK: Ace 7PCD 4406
US: Prestige 4406
**The Complete
Aladdin Recordings**
1992
UK: EMI CDP 7968432
US: EMI USA E22V 96843
Morning Blues *1992*
UK: Charly CDBM 8
Texas Blues Man
1992
UK: Blues Encore CD 52005
**You're Gonna Miss
Me** *1993*
UK: Edsel EDCD 357

**BIG WALTER
"SHAKEY" HORTON**
**Big Walter Horton
With Carey Bell**
1990
UK: Alligator ALCD 4702
US: Alligator ALCD 4702
**Live At The El
Mocambo** *1991*
UK: Red Lightnin' RL CD 0088
**Mouth Harp
Maestro** *1991*
UK: Ace CDCH 252

SON HOUSE
Death Letter *1990*
UK: Edsel EDCD 167
Delta Blues *1991*
US: Biograph BCD 118
**Father Of The Delta
Blues** *1992*
UK: Columbia 4716622

ALBERTA HUNTER
**The Young Alberta
Hunter** *1988*

UK: Jass JASSCD 6
US: Jass JASS 6

IVORY JOE HUNTER
**7th Street Boogie
(1949–50)** *1991*
UK: Mr R&B RBD 7
**I'm Coming Down
With The Blues** *1991*
US: Coll'Bless 5226

**MISSISSIPPI JOHN
HURT**
Avalon Blues
1989
UK: Rounder ROUCD 1081
US: Rounder CD 1081
**Best Of Mississippi
John Hurt**
1991
UK: Vanguard VMCD 7304
US: Vanguard VCD 19
Worried Blues *1992*
UK: Rounder ROUCD 1082
US: Rounder CDROU 1082

ETTA JAMES
Seven Year Itch *1992*
UK: Island CID 1210
US: Island 842655-2
R&B Dynamite *1987*
UK: Ace CDCH 210
US: Virgin V21Z86232
Tell Mama *1992*
UK: Chess CHLD 19035
US: Chess CHD 9269

HOMESICK JAMES
No CDs currently available

SKIP JAMES
The Complete

Recordings *1992*
UK: Great Recording Co
DOCD 5005
**Greatest Of The
Delta Blues Singers**
1992
UK: Biograph BCD 122
US: Biograph 122

**BLIND LEMON
JEFFERSON**
**Blind Lemon
Jefferson (1925–26)**
1991
UK: Document DOCD 5017
**Blind Lemon
Jefferson** *1992*
UK: Ace CDCH 399
US: Milestone MCD 47022

LONNIE JOHNSON
**Me And My Crazy
Self** *1991*
UK: Charly CDCHARLY 266
**Originator Of
Modern Guitar
Blues** *1990*
Sweden: Mr R&B RBD 300
**Steppin' On The
Blues** *1991*
UK: Columbia 4672522

LUTHER JOHNSON
**Take A Bite Outta
The Blues** *1991*
UK: Ichiban ICH 1060CD

ROBERT JOHNSON
**The Complete
Recordings** *1990*
UK: CBS 4672462
US: Columbia CZK 46222

Delta Blues Vol 1
1989
UK: Aldabra ALB 1001 CD
Delta Blues Vol 2
1989
UK: Aldabra ALB 1002CD

TOMMY JOHNSON
**The Complete
Recordings 1928-30**
1990
UK: Wolf WSECD 104

CURTIS JONES
In London *1991*
UK: Limelight 820624 2

JANIS JOPLIN
Pearl/Kosmic Blues
1992
UK: Columbia
Box set 46 10202

LOUIS JORDAN
**Best Of Louis
Jordan** *1991*
US: MCA MCAD4079
**Complete Aladdin
Sessions** *1991*
UK: EMI CZ 426
Golden Greats *1988*
UK: MCA DCML 5005

JO ANNE KELLY
Retrospect 1964–72
1990
UK: Document CSAPCD 101

**KING PLEASURE AND
THE BISCUIT BOYS**
This Is It *1990*
UK: Big Bear BEARCD32

ALBERT KING
Albert *1988*
UK: CHARLY CDCHARLY 103
US: RHINO 70398-2
Best Of Albert King
(I'll Play The Blues
For You/Lovejoy)
1991
UK: STAX CDSX 969
King Does The
King's Thing
(Tribute to Elvis)
1992
UK: STAX CDSXE 073
New Orleans Heat
1987
UK: CHARLY CDCHARLY 49
US: RHINO 70699-2
Truckload Of Lovin'
1988
UK: CHARLY CDCHARLY 112
US: RHINO 70399-2

B. B. KING
Best Of B. B. King
1987
UK: MCA MCLD 19099
US: MCA MCAD 31040
Best Of B. B. King
(Volume 1) *1989*
UK: ACE CDCH 908
Blues Is King *1992*
UK: SEE FOR MILES SEECD 216
US: MCA MCAD 31368
Completely Well
1987
UK: MCA CMCAD 31039
US: MCA MCAD 31039
Do The Boogie
(Early Fifties
Classics) *1988*
UK: ACE CDCH 916

There Is Always
One More Time
1991
UK: MCA MCAD 10295
US: MCA MCAD 10295

EARL KING
Glazed *1988*
US: BLACK TOP CD 1035

FREDDIE KING
Best Of Freddie
King *1991*
US: SHELTER 8010
Burglar *1992*
UK: BEAT GOES ON
BGOCD 137
Getting Ready *1990*
UK: SEQUEL NEXCD 126
Palace Of The King
1991
UK: MAGNUM FORCE
CDBM 089
Takin' Care Of
Business *1986*
UK: CHARLY CDCHARLY 30
Texas Cannonball
1991
UK: SEQUEL NEXCD 175

ALEXIS KORNER
Collection 1961–72
1988
UK: CASTLE COLLECTOR
CCSCD 150
Alexis Korner *1990*
UK: CASTLE CLASSICS
Box set CLABX 914

**ALEXIS KORNER/CYRIL
DAVIES**
Blues Incorporated

1989
UK: LINE TACD9 00634
R&B From The
Marquee *1991*
UK: DERAM 8209862

LAZY LESTER
Harp And Soul *1989*
UK: ALLIGATOR ALCD 4768
US: ALLIGATOR ALCD 7476
Tell Me Pretty Baby
1989
UK: FLYRIGHT FLYCD 07

LEADBELLY
Alabama Bound
1990
UK: BLUEBIRD ND 90321
US: RCA 9600-2
King Of The 12-
String Guitar *1991*
UK: COLUMBIA ROOTS
4678932
US: SONY MUSIC 46776

J. B. LENOIR
J. B. Lenoir *1990*
UK: ROOTS RTS 33027
Alabama Blues *1991*
UK: L&R CDLR 42001
Natural Man *1991*
US: CHESS CHD 9323
Tropical Bluesman
1992
UK: BLUES ENCORE CD 52017

FURRY LEWIS
In His Prime
1927–29
1991
UK: YAZOO YAZCD 12050
US: YAZOO YAZCD 1050

**JOE LIGGINS AND THE
HONEYDRIPPERS**
Joe Liggins and the
Honeydrippers *1990*
UK: ACE CDCHD 307
US: SPECIALTY 7006

MANCE LIPSCOMB
Texas Songster *1992*
US: ARHOOLIE ARH 305

LITTLE SONNY
New King Of The
Blues Harmonica
1991
UK: STAX CDSXD 968

PROFESSOR LONGHAIR
New Orleans
Houseparty
1990
UK: DEMON FIENDCD 189
US: ROUNDER CD2057
Crawfish Fiesta *1992*
UK: ALLIGATOR ALCD 4718
US: ALLIGATOR ALCD 4718

JOE HILL LOUIS
The Be Bop Boy
1992
GERMANY: BEAR FAMILY
BCD 15524

TOMMY McCLENNAN
Travellin' Highway
Man *1990*
UK: TRAVELLIN' MAN TMCD 06

CHARLIE McCOY
Harpin' The Blues
1992
US: SONY MUSIC 47087

JIMMY McCRACKLIN
Everybody Rock!
(Best Of) *1989*
UK: CHARLY CD RED 10
The Mercury
Recordings *1992*
UK: BEAR FAMILY BCD 15558
My Story *1991*
UK: BULLSEYE NETCD 9508
US: BULLSEYE 9508

**MISSISSIPPI FRED
McDOWELL**
Fred McDowell *1990*
UK: FLYRIGHT FLYCD 14
Mississippi Delta
Blues *1992*
US: ARHOOLIE ARH 304

BROWNIE McGHEE
Brownie McGhee
1944–1955 *1990*
UK: TRAVELLIN' MAN
TMCD 004
Folkways Years *1991*
US: FOLKWAYS 40034

BIG JAY McNEELY
Roadhouse Boogie
1991
SWEDEN: SAXOPHONOGRAPH
RBD 505
Swingin' *1991*
US: COLL'BLUES 5133

BLIND WILLIE McTELL
Blind Willie McTell
Vol 1 (1927–31) *1992*
UK: DOCUMENT DOCD 5006
Blind Willie McTell
Vol 2 (1931–32) *1992*
UK: DOCUMENT DOCD 5007

Last Session 1991
US: OR BLUES COJBCD 517 2

TAJ MAHAL
Taj Mahal Collection 1987
UK: CASTLE COLLECTION CCSD 180
Giant Step 1988
UK: EDSEL EDCD 264
US: COLUMBIA 18
Natch'l Blues 1991
UK: EDSEL EDCD 231
Taj Mahal 1988
UK: EDSEL EDCD 166

JOHN MAYALL AND THE BLUESBREAKERS
Bare Wires 1988
UK: LONDON 8205382
Chicago Line 1989
UK: CHARLY CDCHARLY 202
US: ISLAND 842869-2
Crusade 1988
UK: LONDON 8205372

BIG MAYBELLE
The OKeh Sessions 1988
UK: CHARLY CDCHARLY 108

PERCY MAYFIELD
Poet Of The Blues 1990
UK: ACE CDCHD 283
US: SPECIALTY 7001

LITTLE MILTON
Blues In The Night 1992
UK: DILLION 2610 072
Blues 'n' Soul/

Waiting For Little Milton 1992
UK: STAX CDSXD 052
If Walls Could Talk 1991
US: CHESS CHD 9289
TK Sessions 1991
UK: SEQUEL NEXCD 168
We're Gonna Make It 1990
UK: ROOTS RTS 33012

ROY MILTON
Roy Milton And His Solid Senders 1990
UK: ACE CDCHD 308
US: SPECIALTY 7004

CHARLIE MUSSELWHITE
Ace Of Harps 1990
UK: ALLIGATOR ALCD 4781
US: ALLIGATOR ALCD 4781
Mellow Dee 1988
UK: CROSSCUT CCD 11013
Signature 1991
UK: ALLIGATOR ALCD 4801
US: ALLIGATOR ALCD 4801

KENNY NEAL
Devil Child 1988
UK: ALLIGATOR ALCD 4774
US: ALLIGATOR ALCD 4774
Walking On Fire 1991
UK: ALLIGATOR ALCD 4795
US: ALLIGATOR ALCD 4795

RAFUL NEAL
I Been Mistreated 1992
UK: ICHIBAN ICH 9004CD
US: ICHIBAN 9004

ROBERT NIGHTHAWK
Black Angel Blues 1991
UK: CHARLY CDRED 29
Rare Chicago Recordings (Live On Maxwell Street) 1991
UK: ROUNDER CDROU 2022
US: ROUNDER CDROU 2022

JOHNNY OTIS
Creeping With The Cats 1991
UK: ACE CDCHD 325
US: ACE 325
Good Lovin' Blues 1990
UK: ACE CDCH 299
The New Johnny Otis Show 1991
UK: ALLIGATOR ALCD 4726
US: ALLIGATOR ALCD 4726

LITTLE JUNIOR PARKER
Funny How Time Slips Away 1990
US: LRC JAZZ CDC 9002

CHARLIE PATTON
Charlie Patton Vol 1 (1929) 1992
UK: DOCUMENT DOCD 5009
Charlie Patton Vol 2 (1929) 1992
UK: DOCUMENT DOCD 5010
Charlie Patton Vol 3 (1929–34) 1992
UK: DOCUMENT DOCD 5011

PINETOP PERKINS
Pinetop's Boogie

Woogie 1992
UK: ANTONE'S ANTCD 0020
US: ANTONE'S 20

LUCKY PETERSON
Lucky Strikes 1989
UK: ALLIGATOR ALCD 4770
US: ALLIGATOR ALCD 4770
Triple Play 1991
UK: ALLIGATOR ALCD 4789
US: ALLIGATOR ALCD 4789

SNOOKY PRYOR
Too Cool To Move 1991
UK: ANTONE'S ANTCD 17
US: ANTONE'S 17

QUEEN IDA
Cookin' With Queen Ida 1989
UK: SONET SNCD 1021
US: GNP CR6SC 2197

MA RAINEY
Ma Rainey's Black Bottom 1991
UK: VIRGIN CDV 2659
US: YAZOO YAZCD 1071

BONNIE RAITT
Collection 1990
UK: WARNER BROS 7599262422
US: WARNER BROS 262422

LOUISIANA RED
Blues For Ida B 1988
UK: JSP CD209
Lowdown Back Porch Blues 1992
UK: SEQUEL NEXCD 213

SPECKLED RED
NO CDS CURRENTLY AVAILABLE

A. C. REED
I'm In The Wrong Business 1992
UK: ALLIGATOR ALCD 4757
US: ALLIGATOR ALCD 4757

JIMMY REED
Big Boss Blues 1986
UK: CHARLY CDCHARLY 3
Big Boss Man 1991
UK: INSTANT CDINS 5042
Greatest Hits 1991
US: HOLLYWOOD 445
Jimmy Reed 1990
UK: FLYRIGHT FLYCD 15
Rockin' With Reed 1987
UK: CHARLY CDCHARLY 61

TOMMY RIDGLEY
New Orleans King Of The Stroll 1990
US: ROUNDER CD2079

FENTON ROBINSON
I Hear Some Blues Downstairs 1991
UK: ALLIGATOR ALCD 4710
US: ALLIGATOR ALCD 4710
Sings The Blues 1990
UK: SEQUEL NEXCD 142
That's All Right 1989
UK: CHARLY CDRED 16
(DELETED 1990)

ROLLING STONES
Rolling Stones 1985
UK: LONDON 8200472
US: ABKCO CD7375

**The Rolling Stones
Now** *1988*
UK: LONDON 8201332
US: ABKCO 7420-2

BOBBY RUSH
I Ain't Studdin You
1991
UK: URGENT URG 4117 CD
US: URGENT 4117

OTIS RUSH
Classic Recordings
1990
UK: CHARLY CDCHARLY 217
**Cobra Recordings
1956–58** *1988*
UK: FLYRIGHT FLYCD 01
US: PAULA JWL 1
Lost In The Blues
1991
UK: SONET SNTCD 1045
**Right Place Wrong
Time** *1991*
UK: EDSEL EDCD 220
US: HIGHTONE 8007

JIMMY RUSHING
Two Shades Of Blue
1992
UK: TKO TKOCD 022
**The You And Me
That Used To Be**
1989
UK: BLUEBIRD ND 86460
US: BLUEBIRD 64602

MAGIC SAM
Easy Baby *1990*
UK: CHARLY CDCHARLY 218
**Late Great Magic
Sam** *1991*

US: L&R 2014
Westside Guitar
1989
UK: FLYRIGHT FLYCD 02
US: PAULA JWL 2

SON SEALS
Bad Axe *1992*
UK: ALLIGATOR ALCD 4738
US: ALLIGATOR ALCD 4738
**Living In The
Danger Zone** *1991*
UK: ALLIGATOR ALCD 4798
US: ALLIGATOR ALCD 4798

J. D. SHORT
Legacy Of The Blues
1991
UK: SONET SNTCD 648

NINA SIMONE
Best Of Nina Simone
1990
UK: ND 90378
US: RCA 4374-2
Sings The Blues
1991
UK: NOVUS ND83101
US: NOVUS 31012
**The Nina Simone
Story** *1989*
UK: DEJA VU DVRECD 15

GUITAR SLIM
Story Of My Life
1992
UK: SKY RANCH SR 652311
US: ORLEANS 4188
**Things That I Used
To Do**
1991
UK: ACE CDCHD 318

LIGHTNING SLIM
Blue Lightning *1992*
UK: INDIGO IGOCD 2002
**King Of The Swamp
Blues 1958–64** *1992*
UK: FLYRIGHT FLYCD 47
Rollin' Stone *1989*
UK: FLYRIGHT FLYCD 08

MEMPHIS SLIM
All Kinds Of Blues
1987
US:OR BLUES COJBCD 507–2
**The Memphis Slim
Story** *1989*
UK: DEJA VU DVRECD 18
Real Folk Blues *1991*
US: MCA MCAD 9270
Rockin' The Blues
1990
UK: CHARLY CDCHARLY 210
Worried Life *1990*
UK: ROOTS RTS 33013
**You Got To Help
Me Some** *1992*
UK: BLUES ENCORE CD 52013

SUNNYLAND SLIM
NO CDs CURRENTLY AVAILABLE

BESSIE SMITH
**The Complete
Collection Vol 1**
1991
UK: COLUMBIA BOX SET
4678952
US: SONY MUSIC 47091
**The Complete
Collection Vol 2**
1991
UK: COLUMBIA BOX SET
4687672

US: SONY MUSIC 47471
**The Greatest Blues
Singer In The World**
1992
UK: BLUES ENCORE CD 52009
20 Golden Greats
1987
UK: DEJA VU DVCD 2008

BYTHER SMITH
House Fire *1991*
UK: BULLSEYE NETCD 9503
US: BULLSEYE 9503

LITTLE GEORGE SMITH
Harmonica Ace *1991*
UK: ACE CDCHD 337

VICTORIA SPIVEY
NO CDs CURRENTLY AVAILABLE

FRANK STOKES
**Creator Of The
Memphis Blues** *1991*
UK: YAZOO YAZCD 1056
US: YAZOO YAZ 1056
**The Victor
Recordings** *1992*
UK: DOCUMENT DOCD 5013

ROOSEVELT SYKES
Goldmine *1990*
US: DELMARK 616
The Honeydripper
1992
UK: BLUES ENCORE CD 52014

HOUND DOG TAYLOR
Natural Boogie *1990*
UK: ALLIGATOR ALCD 4704
US: ALLIGATOR ALCD 4704
Genuine House

Rocking Music *1991*
UK: ALLIGATOR ALCD 4727
US: ALLIGATOR ALCD 1727
Beware Of The Dog
1991
UK: ALLIGATOR ALCD 4707
US: ALLIGATOR ALCD 4707

**JESSE "GUITAR"
TAYLOR**
Last Night *1990*
UK: BEDROCK BEDCO 14

JOHNNIE TAYLOR
Raw Blues *1991*
US: STAX SCD 8508
**Raw Blues/Little
Bluebird** *1992*
UK: STAX CDSXD 051

**LITTLE JOHNNY
TAYLOR**
Part Time Love *1987*
UK: CHRIS WELLARD CD 229
The Galaxy Years
1991
UK: ACE CDCHD 967
Greatest Hits *1990*
US: FANTASY FCD 4510

KOKO TAYLOR
**From The Heart Of
A Woman** *1990*
UK: ALLIGATOR ALCD 4724
US: ALLIGATOR ALCD 4724
I Got What It Takes
1991
UK: ALLIGATOR ALCD 4706
US: ALLIGATOR ALCD 4706
Koko Taylor *1990*
US: CHESS CHD 31271
Love You Like A

Woman *1990*
UK: CHESS CDRED 25

SONNY TERRY AND BROWNIE McGHEE
Back To New Orleans *1992*
UK: ACE CDCH 372
Hometown Blues *1991*
UK: MAINSTREAM MDCD 902
Midnight Special *1990*
UK: ACE CDCH 951
US: FANTASY FCD 24721
Sonny And Brownie *1989*
UK: A&M CDA 0829
US: A&M CD 0829

HENRY THOMAS
The Complete Recordings *1991*
UK: YAZOO YAZCD 1080
US: YAZOO YAZCD 1080

WILLIE MAE "BIG MAMA" THORNTON
The Original Hound Dog *1990*
UK: ACE CDCHD 940
Jail *1990*
US: VANGUARD VCD 79351

TOMMY TUCKER
No CDs CURRENTLY AVAILABLE

IKE TURNER
Ike Turner *1991*
US: PAULA 16
1958–59 Titles For Cobra And Artistic

1991
UK: FLYRIGHT FLYCD 39
Rock Me Baby (with Tina Turner) *1987*
UK: TOPLINE TOPCD 511
Trailblazer *1991*
UK: CHARLY CDCHARLY 263

BIG JOE TURNER
The Blues Boss *1992*
UK: BLUES ENCORE CD52008
Boss Of The Blues *1990*
UK: ATLANTIC K781 459 2
Every Day I Have The Blues *1991*
US: OR JAZZ CL OJCCD 6342
I Don't Dig It *1991*
UK: MR R&B 618

STEVIE RAY VAUGHAN
Sky Is Crying *1991*
UK: EPIC 4655712
US: SONY MUSIC 47390
Texas Flood *1991*
UK: EPIC CD 460951
US: EPIC 38734

EDDIE "CLEANHEAD" VINSON
Back In Town *1987*
UK: CHARLY CDCHARLY 50
Cleanhead And Cannonball (with Cannonball Adderley) *1988*
US: LANDMARK LCD 13092

LITTLE WALTER
Blues With A Feeling *1992*

UK: DILLION 26 10 082
Best Of Little Walter *1991*
US: CHESS CHD 9192
Boss Blues Harmonica *1988*
UK: CHARLY CDRED 4

WASHBOARD SAM
Rocking My Blues Away *1992*
UK: BLUEBIRD ND 90652
US: RCA 610422

DINAH WASHINGTON
Bessie Smith Songbook *1986*
UK: MERCURY 826 663-2
US: POLYGRAM 826663-2
Best Of Dinah Washington *1992*
UK: ROULETTE CDROU 1054

WALTER "WOLFMAN" WASHINGTON
Out Of The Dark *1988*
UK: ROUNDER CD 2068
US: ROUNDER CD 2068
Wolf Tracks *1988*
UK: ROUNDER CD 2048
US: ROUNDER CD 2048

ETHEL WATERS
On Stage And Screen 1925–40 *1990*
US: CSP 2792
Push Out *1991*
UK: ZETA ZET 747

MUDDY WATERS
20 Blues Greats *1987*

UK: DEJA VU DVCD 2034
Chess Box Set *1990*
UK: MCA BOX set CHD 380002
US: CHESS BOX set CHD3 80002
Father Of Chicago Blues *1992*
UK: BLUES ENCORE CD 52001
Fathers And Sons *1988*
UK: CHESS CDR6D8
Muddy Waters Anthology *1991*
UK: PLATINUM MUSIC PLATCD 3911

JOHNNY "GUITAR" WATSON
I Heard That *1987*
UK: CHARLY CDCHARLY 38
Three Hours Past Midnight *1987*
UK: ACE CDCH 909
US: VIRGIN V21Y 86233

JUNIOR WELLS
It's My Life Baby *1989*
UK: START VMCD 7311
US: VANGUARD VCD 73120
Messin' With The Kid *1990*
UK: CHARLY CDCHARLY 219
US: PAULA JWL 3

BUKKA WHITE
Complete Sessions (1930–1940) *1990*
UK: TRAVELIN' MAN TMCD 03
Sky Songs *1991*
US: ARHOOLIE 323

BIG JOE WILLIAMS
1935–41 Vol 1 *1991*
UK: BLUES DOCUMENT BDCD 6003
1945–49 Vol 2 *1991*
UK: BLUES DOCUMENT BDCD 6004
Blues On Highway 49 *1990*
US: DELMARK 604
Hand Me Down My Old Walking Stick *1992*
UK: SEQUEL NEXCD 208

JOE WILLIAMS
Nothin' But The Blues *1986*
UK: DELOS DCD 4001
US: DELOS DCD 4001

JOHN LEE "SONNY BOY" WILLIAMSON
Throw A Boogie *1990*
UK: BLUEBIRD ND 90320
US: BLUEBIRD 95992

SONNY BOY WILLIAMSON II (RICE MILLER)
The Best Of Sonny Boy Williamson *1991*
UK: CHARLY CDRED 23
The Blues Of Sonny Boy Williamson *1987*
UK: STORYVILLE STCD 4062
The Chess Years *1991*
UK: CHARLY BOX set CDRED BOX 1
Down And Out

Blues 1990
UK: Chess CHD 31272
US: Chess CHCD 80

CHICK WILLIS
Now 1989
UK: Ichiban CDICH 1029

JOHNNY WINTER
Johnny Winter
Collection 1988
UK: Castle Collector
CCSCD 167
Living In The Blues
1992
UK: Thunderbolt CDTB 083
Third Degree 1986
UK: Alligator ALCD 4748
US: Alligator ALCD 4748

JIMMY WITHERSPOON
Baby Baby Baby
1990
US: Or Blues COJBCD 527 2
Blues, The Whole
Blues And Nothing
But The Blues 1992
UK: Indigo IGOCD 2001
Blowin' In From
Kansas City 1991
UK: Ace CDCHD 279
Jay's Blues 1991
UK: Charly CDCHARLY 270

HOWLIN' WOLF
Chess Box 1991
US: MCA CHD 3-9332
Howlin' Wolf
Collection 1990
UK: Deja Vu DVCD 2032
Memphis Days 1989
UK: Bear Family

BCD 15460
Moanin' Moonlight
1990
US: Chess CHD 5908
The Power Of The
Voice 1990
UK: Blues Encore CD 52002
Rides Again 1991
UK: Ace CDCHD 333
Wolf Is At Your
Door 1992
UK: Charly CD BM 5

JIMMY YANCEY
Volume 1 (1939–40)
1992
UK: Document DOCD 5041
Volume 2 (1940–43)
1992
UK: Document DOCD 5043
Volume 3 (1943–50)
1992
UK: Document DOCD 5044

MIGHTY JOE YOUNG
Bluesy Josephine
1991
UK: Black & Blue BLE 595212

COMPILATIONS

20 Great Blues
Recordings Of The
Fifties And Sixties
1990
Lightnin' Hopkins; Bobby
"Blue" Bland; Roosevelt
Sykes; Big Mama
Thornton; Jimmy
Witherspoon; Sonny Boy
Williamson; John Lee

Hooker; Elmore James;
Howlin' Wolf; B. B. King;
Johnny "Guitar" Watson;
Jimmy McCracklin; Lowell
Fulsom, etc.
UK: Cascade CDROP 1005

60 Great Blues
Recordings Of The
Fifties And Sixties
1990
Extended CD box set of
the above.
UK: Cascade BOX SET
CBOCD3

Beauty Of The Blues
1991
Robert Johnson; Big Three
Trio; Lonnie Johnson; Big
Bill Broonzy; Bessie Smith;
Big Joe Williams; Blind
Boy Fuller; Memphis
Minnie; Leadbelly; Jazz
Gillum; Blind Willie
McTell; Willie Smith, etc.
UK: Columbia 4687682
US: Sony Music 47465

Best Of Chess
Blues: 1 1989
Otis Rush; Sonny Boy
Williamson; Muddy
Waters; Howlin' Wolf;
Eddie Boyd; Chuck Berry;
Lowell Fulsom; Willie
Dixon; Albert King;
Memphis Slim; Buddy Guy;
Willie Mabon; Jimmy
Witherspoon; John Lee
Hooker, etc.
UK: Charly CDRED 11

Best Of The Blues
Singers 1989
Ray Charles; Muddy
Waters; T-Bone Walker;
Joe Williams; Big Joe
Turner; Little Junior
Parker.
UK: Denon DC 8530
US: Legacy 348

Beware Of The
Texas Blues (Vol 1)
1991
Guitar Slim; Johnny
Copeland; Big Walter;
Clarence Green; Eastwood
Review; Freeze.
UK: Blue Moon CDBM 064
Beware Of The
Texas Blues (Vol 2)
1991
UK: Blue Moon CDBM 085

Blow It 'Till You
Like It 1990
Walter "Shakey" Horton;
Dr Isaiah Ross; Houston
Boines; Coy "Hot Shot"
Love; Joe Hill Louis;
Woodrow Adams; Willie
Nix.
UK: Sun CD Sun 27

The Blues—A Real
Summit Meeting
1988
Big Mama Thornton; Eddie
"Cleanhead" Vinson; Arthur
"Big Boy" Crudup; Lloyd
Glen; Muddy Waters;
Clarence Brown; B. B.
King; Jay McShann.

UK: Charly CDCHARLY 135

Blues Came Down
From Memphis 1987
Joe Hill Louis; Rufus
Thomas; Dr Isaiah Ross;
Jimmy Deberry; Walter
"Shakey" Horton; Willie
Nix; James Cotton; Little
Junior Parker; Houston
Boines; Sonny Lewis;
Willie Johnson.
UK: Charly CDCHARLY 67

Blues From
Dolphins Of
Hollywood 1991
Pee Wee Crayton; Little
Caesar; Percy Mayfield;
Jimmy Witherspoon;
Peppermint Harris; Floyd
Dixon.
UK: Ace CDCH 357

Blues Guitar Box
1990
T-Bone Walker; John
Mayall's Bluesbreakers;
Allman Brothers Band; B.
B. King; Mike Bloomfield;
Albert King; Roy
Buchanan; Clarence
"Gatemouth" Brown;
Albert King; Otis Rush;
Muddy Waters; Albert
Collins; Hound Dog
Taylor; Robert Cray; Little
Milton, etc.
UK: Sequel BOX SET
TBBCD 47555

Blues Round

Midnight *1988*
Larry Davis; Johnny Copeland; Lowell Fulsom; T-Bone Walker, B. B. King; Ray Charles; Jimmy Nelson; Saunders King; Frankie Ervin; Marti Jones; Lorenzo Holden; Jimmy Witherspoon; Vivianne Green.
UK: Ace CDCH 235

Bluestream (The Best Of Mainstream Blues) *1991*
John Lee Hooker; Lightnin' Hopkins; Sonny Terry & Brownie McGhee; Peppermint Harris; Roscoe Gordon; Smokey Hogg; Ray Charles; James Wayne; R. B. Stidham.
UK: Mainstream MNCD 904
US: Mainstream 904

Bluesville (Vol 1) *1988*
Furry Lewis; K.C.Douglas; Big Joe Williams; Blind Willie McTell; Lonnie Johnson; Scrapper Blackwell; Revd Blind Gary Davis; Snooks Eaglin; Sonny Terry & Brownie McGhee; Lightnin' Hopkins, etc.
UK: Ace CDCH 247

Bluesville (Vol 2) *1988*
Eddie Kirkland; Homesick James; Memphis Slim; Lightnin' Hopkins; Sonny

Terry; Billy Boy Arnold; Roosevelt Sykes; Buddy Lucas; Jimmy Witherspoon; King Curtis.
UK: Ace CDCH 250

Boogie Woogie Blues *1991*
Cow Cow Davenport; James P. Johnson; Clarence Williams; Clarence Johnson; Jimmy Blyth; Everett Robbins; Hersal Thomas; Lemuel Fowler.
US: Biograph BCD 118

Chicago Blues *1989*
Buddy Guy; Junior Wells; Johnny Young; Muddy Waters; Mighty Joe Young; Koko Taylor; J. B. Hutto; Johnny Lewis.
UK: Red Lightnin' RLCD 0080

Demon Blues *1992*
Joe Louis Walker; Phillip Walker; George Thorogood And The Destroyers; Hubert Sumlin; Duke Robilliard; Professor Longhair; Earl King; John Lee Hooker; John Hammond; Rory Gallagher; Snooks Eaglin; Dr John, etc.
UK: Demon FIENDCD 714

Gin House Blues *1992*
Mamie Smith; Margaret Johnson; Bessie Smith; Lether McGraw; Margaret

Johnson; Edna Winston; Rosetta Howard; Trixie Smith; Rosetta Crawford; Babe Hines.
UK: Flapper PASTCD 9788

Good Time Blues: Harmonica, Kazoos, Washboards And Cowbells *1991*
Mississippi Jook Band; Memphis Jug Band; Son Becky; Charlie And His Memphis Mudcats; Georgia Brown; Big Joe And His Washboard Band; Buddy Lucas; Peter Chatman; Sonny Terry; Jordan Webb; Bernice Edwards.
UK: Columbia 4678912
US: Sony Music 46780

Instant Blues *1989*
Albert King; Robert Cray; John Lee Hooker; Elmore James; Little Walter; Lowell Fulsom; Junior Wells; Howlin' Wolf; Otis Rush; T-Bone Walker; Buddy Guy.
UK: Instant CDINS 5011

Kings Of The Blues *1989*
B. B. King; Johnny "Guitar" Watson; Frankie Lee Sims; Baby Face Turner; John Lee Hooker; T-Bone Walker; Mercy Dee; Bumble Bee Slim; Chuck Higgins; Pee Wee Crayton; Smokey Hogg;

Lowell Fulsom; Eddie "Guitar" Burns; Lightnin' Hopkins; Clifton Chenier; Elmore James; Floyd Dixon.
UK: Ace CDCH 276

This Is The Blues *1990*
Bo Diddley; Howlin' Wolf; Sonny Boy Williamson; Etta James; Chuck Berry; Muddy Waters; Wilbert Harrison; Jimmy Reed; John Lee Hooker; Albert King; Tommy Tucker.
UK: Platinum Music PLATCD 3909

Chicago Guitars *1990*
Buddy Guy; Otis Rush; Magic Sam.
UK: Flyright FLYCD 18

Canned Heat Blues: Masters Of The Delta Blues *1992*
Furry Lewis; Tommy Johnson; Ishman Bracey.
UK: Bluebird ND 90648
US: RCA 61047-2

Good Morning Blues *1991*
Leadbelly; Dan Smith; Revd Blind Gary Davis.
US: Biograph BCD 113

Nasty Blues *1989*
Clarence Carter; Trudy

Lynn; Artie White; Gary B. B. Coleman; Chick Willis; Little Johnny Taylor; Travis Haddix.
UK: Ichiban ICH 1048 CD
US: Ichiban ICH 1048 CD

Newport In New York *1991*
B. B. King; Lloyd Glen; Big Mama Thornton; Clarence "Gatemouth" Brown; Muddy Waters.
UK: Blue Moon CDBM 071
US: Magnum 7071

Sun Blues Archives Vol 1 *1990*
Earl Hooker; Pinetop Perkins; Lewis Johnson; Coy Love; Pat Hare; L. B. Lawson.
UK: Sun CDSUN 29

Sun Blues Archives Vol 2 *1990*
Roscoe Gordon; Red Guitars; Junior Parker; Elven Parr; Eddie Snow.
UK: Sun CDSUN 30

This Is Black Top *1989*
Anson Funderburgh; Sam Myers; Earl King; Snooks Eaglin; Neville Brothers; Bobby Radcliff; Hubert Sumlin; Mighty Sam; Grady Gaines; Joe Medwick; Ron Levy; James "Thunderbird" Davis.
UK: Demon BTSCD 1
(deleted 1991)

index

142

acknowledgements

Photographs reproduced by kind permission of London Features International/Nick Elgar, Jan Goedefroit, Mark Hadley, Michel Linssen, Michael Ochs Archive, Ken Regan, Aubrey Reuben and Kristin Vraa.

Front jacket: Retna/M. Putland.
Back jacket: Rex Features, Retna/Jay Blakesberg, Pictorial Press, Pictorial Press/Keuntje, Rex Features.